A Discourse on Meekness

and Quietness of Spirit
Rewalked

Rewritten in Modern English by

Shawn P. Robinson

A Modern-Day Retelling of Matthew Henry's Classic

BrainSwell

BrainSwell Publishing
Ingersoll, Ontario

Original version published by The American Tract Society in 1836.
Matthew Henry (18 October 1662 – 22 June 1714)

A meek and quiet spirit, which is in the sight of God of great price.
1 Peter 3:4

Dedication

To my dear wife, Juanita, who not only loves this book, but has been hoping I would do a contemporary rewrite of it for a long time.

To our good friend, Nicole, who introduced this much needed book to my wife and, through her, to me.

To all believers everywhere who will benefit from a moment to consider this beautiful adornment of meekness.

Books by
Shawn P. B. Robinson

Christian Discipleship

Pilgrim's Progress *Rewalked*
Pilgrim's Progress *Rewalked* with Study Guide
Pilgrim's Progress Annotated Original with Study Guide
A Discourse on Meekness and Quietness of Spirit *Rewalked*

Adult Fiction (Sci-fi & Fantasy)

The Ridge Series (3 books)
ADA: An Anthology of Short Stories

YA Fiction (Fantasy, Sci-fi, Dystopian)

The Sevordine Chronicles (5 Books)
Greks (2 Books)—Coming Soon
The Modder's Run (2 Books)—Coming Soon

Books for Younger Readers

Jerry the Squirrel (4 Books)
Arestana Series (3 Books)
Annalynn the Canadian Spy Series (6 Books)
Activity Books (2 Books)

www.shawnpbrobinson.com/books

Table of Contents

Introduction

In the final years of the 17th century, Matthew Henry shared this powerful discourse on meekness, and it was later put down into a book, allowing many others to benefit from it beyond those in the original audience. The challenge for us, of course, is that Henry wrote this over three hundred years ago, and the English language has gone through some significant renovations since that time. As such, the meanings of many words have changed, many words have fallen out of use, and the style of writing, the forming of sentences, and more have all radically changed.

The result is his original Discourse on Meekness and Gentleness of Spirit has grown quite difficult to read. Now, if you're used to reading older English, you may not struggle like most readers, but for the rest of us, my hope is a contemporary rewrite might be just what we need to expose the Christian church to this much needed teaching.

I wish, in this Introduction, to share a little of the approach taken to this *Rewalked* edition. This is part of a larger series of modern-day rewrites that began a while back with Pilgrim's Progress. Lord willing, I will have the chance to do some more of these as time goes on, but that's in the Lord's hands and plans, not mine.

In working through the book, I attempted, as best I could, to maintain an accurate rewrite of M. Henry's work. Unfortunately, this means that at times some of his beautiful writing was "lost in translation" but I have attempted to keep the flow as much as possible.

I also found that there were different versions of this book. There is a *fuller* version that includes everything I suspect he originally intended to be in this discourse. This fuller version appears in two forms, one a little harder to read than the other, and I have not been able to identify what happened there. I suspect someone rewrote the original version at some point and added mistakes (unintentionally, I assume) as well as changed some of the wording and spelling.

There is also an abridged version that has removed some of the more difficult statements, the occasional sentence, phrase, or paragraph, his introduction (which I have renamed *The Grace of Meekness*), and his personal note to the readers. In working with these, I have tried to add it all back in, sometimes right into the text, at other times as a footnote. Amidst this process, there were times I thought, "I see why someone took that out," simply because of how confusing the wording was, and at other times, I do not know why it was removed other than for the purpose of shortening the text. Also, I would not be in the least surprised if I have missed portions of the text. This was not an easy process.

In the footnotes, I have included not only notes about missing sections of the book, but I have also included the occasional note to indicate the original wording of a sentence. I did this whenever I was not entirely convinced I had rewritten the section properly. Some of Henry's sentences were filled with so many unusual words, words that had changed meaning, and were organised in such a confusing order that I was left scratching my head as to what he could possibly mean. I leave these sentences to you to evaluate if the *Rewalked* edition is accurate.

Also, in the footnotes, I have added citations to quotes within this work. Henry referenced numerous people from Seneca the Younger to Thomas Linacre,[1] and as best as I was

---

[1] In the back matter of this book, I have included a list of authors Henry quoted along with when they lived, where they lived, and what they did/were known for.

able, I tracked down these references and included not only the name of the book/writing, but also a link to the location for this book online.

Sadly, this was also not an easy process. Henry makes many references without actually saying who he is quoting, and he often does not quote word-for-word. Since he regularly paraphrases those he is quoting, there were times I simply could not find the quote but found rather a section of the book that I believe he summed up or paraphrased. If, while reading, you recognise something I have missed in terms of a quote of someone or if you find a mistake, please contact me, so I can fill in that detail.

When creating footnotes, there were times I shared something of my own thoughts. Often this information is indicated by the addition of the phrase, *SPR Note*. This does not include translations of quotes which I tracked down, websites found, or the occasional comment when referencing primary or translated sources.

Henry also uses a great deal of Scripture, enough that I have been provoked to envy as I see how well he knew the Bible, especially considering how much younger he was when he wrote this book than I am now. The challenge, however, is that he did not always give a Scripture reference for his quotes, nor did he always make it clear he was quoting Scripture.

I have attempted to track down as many of these references as I can and put them in the footnotes, however, I strongly suspect that I have missed more than a few. If you find references I have missed, please contact me and point it out. Despite the fact that I have added in literally hundreds of references, I would not be surprised to discover that there are hundreds more that I have missed.

I have primarily used the ESV translation for these references and in rewriting sentences, however, at times the difference between the KJV and ESV were significant, and I had to use the KJV to maintain Henry's argument. Whenever I did this, I indicated it in the text or footnotes.

The original version also included many Greek and Latin references (even one or two in Hebrew). I have occasionally included forms of this, translated it at other times, once or twice left it in the main body of the text, and at other times made great use of the footnotes to tie it all together. The decisions I made in each circumstance were for the balance of readability (since few of us read Biblical Greek, Hebrew, or ancient Latin) and education, hoping there will be those who appreciate the greater detail.

At times, I not only reworded the book, but I tried to contemporize some concepts. Henry often refers to *masters* and *servants*, but this is not a dynamic we hold to in contemporary western culture. As such, I often used terms like *employers* and *employees* in place of this wording.

There was once or twice where I briefly explained some detail in Greek or Hebrew. Hebrew was never my strong point, although I did a great deal of study in Greek. However, that was not only years ago, but I have, I must confess, had a serious brain trauma since that point. As such, digging up of my old, rusty Greek knowledge from the dark ages was admittedly both fun and challenging. If you find my simple comments less than scholarly, please let me know, and I will seek to meekly respond and adjust.

Henry also felt that the longest run-on sentence told by a four-year-old relaying his experience at a park truly is child's play. As such, I think if he could, he would have made this entire book one sentence and, of course, one, single paragraph. I have tried to break up many of his sentences so that the reader can finish, at the very least, one sentence in a single reading, but I was not always successful.

In the end, I truly hope this *Rewalked* edition will be a blessing and a help to you in your walk with Christ.

God bless you,

Shawn P. Robinson

Preface

We live in a time where everyone and everything around us appears to pursue power. Everything is about *my* choice, *my* rights, *my* feelings. If you want something, the world tells you the best thing (and the most moral thing) you can do is to pursue and attain it.

But then, as followers of Jesus, we read of this concept of meekness, and we find ourselves questioning if this pursuit of power and control over our lives is truly what God has called us to. Now, meekness stands in contrast to this pursuit of power, this desire to stand tall and have everything we want. It is not that a meek man gives up all power, but that a meek man finds a new posture, one of sacrifice, one of internal control, one of thoughtful, prayerful, and humble contentedness in the power of Christ.

I wonder to myself what the church would be like if meekness was as highly esteemed as the other important things we pursue, such as solid teaching, powerful worship, leadership, and good coffee.[2] How would meekness affect our interactions, our leadership processes, dealing with conflicts, sharing the gospel, taking a stand on social issues, and more? I suspect every one of these areas would be greatly transformed!

In this book, Matthew Henry brilliantly lays out an argument for Christian meekness as commanded in Scripture

---

[2] SPR Note: Please excuse my tongue-in-cheek reference to this *evangelistic* approach from yesteryear.

and illustrated powerfully for us through the saints of old, and, of course, through our Lord and Saviour Jesus Christ.

Now, as for me, a while back, my wife (through a friend) came across an early version of this book and found herself amazed not only by the beautiful writing, but also by the powerful message contained within. She became convinced this was a message the Christian church needed to hear today, and I suspect part of the reason she encouraged me to do this rewrite is because she strongly felt I needed to hear this message as well.

I will confess, it is true. This is a message I needed—and continue to need—and I truly hope you will be blessed by the timeless truths contained within this book.

Shawn P. Robinson

Note to the Reader

From Matthew Henry

I do not think[3] it at all needful to tell the world what it was which led me to the writing of this discourse concerning Meekness, the substance of which was preached several years ago; nor am I concerned to apologize for the publication of it: if I thought it needed an apology I would not consent to it. That temper of mind, which it endeavours to promote, and to charm men into, every one will own to be highly conducive to the comfort of human life, the honour of our holy religion, and the welfare and happiness of all societies, civil and sacred: and therefore, while the design cannot be disliked, I hope what is weak and defective in the management, will be excused.

Some useful discourses have been of late published against rash anger, and an excellent dissuasive from revenge by the present Bishop of Chester;[4] wherein those brutish vices are justly exposed. I am cooperating in the design, while I recommend the contrary virtues to the love and practice of all that profess relation to the Holy Jesus. And if this Essay have

---

[3] SPR NOTE: I chose not to rewrite this note *To the Reader* from Matthew Henry in modern English as I thought something very personal and direct as this might be best said in Matthew Henry's own words.

[4] Bishop Nicholas Stratford (1633-1708), who served as Bishop of Chester from 1689 to 1707.

that good effect upon those into whose hands it shall at any time fall, my object will be attained.

As to the Sermon annexed, it is published (with some enlargements) at the request of a very worthy friend who heard it preached in London last summer: and since, blessed be God, there are a great many testimonies borne at this day, against the avowed infidelity and impiety of the age, I hope this may be accepted as a mite cast into that treasury, by a cordial friend to peace and holiness.

Chester, Nov. 21, 1698.

Intro: The Grace of Meekness

"But let your adorning be the hidden person of
the heart with the imperishable beauty of a
gentle and quiet spirit, which in God's sight is
very precious."

1 Peter 3:4

The Apostle Peter[5] in this epistle (as also his beloved
brother Paul in many of his) is very focused on pushing
Christians in the area of the conscientious effort needed to
relate properly with one another. Here he is, in the early part
of this chapter,[6] directing Christian wives to carry themselves
in their context to the glory of God, their own comfort, and
the spiritual benefit and advantage of their husbands.

Paul also teaches them how to dress themselves as
"proper for women who profess godliness."[7] Those of the

---

[5] Not all original versions include this Introduction.

[6] 1 Peter 3:1-2.

[7] 1 Timothy 2:10. SPR Note: In the original version, M. Henry uses the
pronoun "he" in this spot which seems to refer to Peter, but I have changed
this to Paul as it fits the reference. Note from some versions: φιλόκοσμον.
The race of women is attached to ornaments. Lorin. in loc. This appears to be a
reference from Commentaria in Sacram Scripturam by Joannes Lorinus, a
17th century Jesuit and theologian.

fairer sex are often observed to be very concerned about their jewelry and makeup. When the question is asked, "Can a virgin forget her ornaments, or a bride her attire?"[8] It is assumed the answer is a most definite "No!".

The Apostle Peter focuses in on this strong inclination as he recommends the graces and duties of meekness to women's choices and activities, which are certainly the most wonderful and pleasing means to adorn themselves. Of course, this grace of meekness is not only for women, to whom the passage is primarily written, but it is no doubt also directed to men.

Consider the method the Apostle takes:

First, Turn Away from Outward Adornments

Peter endeavours to wean them off the vanity of outward adornments, "Do not let your adorning be external."[9] This does not, of course, forbid the restrained and moderate use of decent jewelry and makeup, when it is according to the social status, place, station,[10] and at an appropriate time,[11] but it forbids the unrestrained love and excessive use[12] of them.

There may be the braiding of hair and the putting on of gold jewelry, and there must be the putting on of clothes, a necessary act due to the effect of sin causing shame as it came into the world. However, we must not make these things *our adorning*, that is we must not set our hearts upon them, nor should we ever see our personal value as tied to them, nor

---

[8] Jeremiah 2:32.

[9] 1 Peter 3:3. ων ἰσω-κόσμος. SPR Note: this Greek phrase would point to keeping your *adorning* appropriate/balanced/moderate.

[10] Original: *quality, place, and station.* All three words point somewhat to the concept of social status.

[11] *Not on days of fasting and humiliation when it is proper for ornaments to be set aside.* Exodus 33:4-5.

[12] *...or abuse...*

should we pride ourselves in them as if they added any real value to us, nor should we say to them as Saul did to Samuel, "honour me now before the elders of my people and before Israel."[13] Saul said this out of a vain ambition to make a himself look good before others.

We must spend no more care, thought, time, words, or cost about these things, and lay no more stress or weight upon them than they deserve—and they deserve very little! It is nothing more than glory hanging on our bodies, just as we see in Isaiah 22:24, "and they will hang on him the whole honor of his father's house." This is nothing compared to the excellent glory that belongs to the creation far below us, for "even Solomon in all his glory was not arrayed" or made beautiful like one of the lilies of the field which exists today and is thrown into the oven tomorrow.[14]

We must not seek these things *first,* nor should we ever seek them *most,* as if we have bodies for no other reason than to cover them with clothing and have no purpose for them other than to make them look pretty.

In the parable of Lazarus and the Rich Man, it was not only foolishness, but the Rich Man's focus on his purple clothing, fine linen, and good things that proved to be the ruin of him. These were the things upon which he placed his happiness and comfort.[15] He made these things his covering, and when he was left without them, he was found naked.[16]

Do not let the wearing of gold and the putting on of nice clothing to be your entire world.[17] More than that, these things

---

[13] 1 Samuel 15:30.

[14] Matthew 6:28-30.

[15] Luke 16:19, 25.

[16] 2 Corinthians 5:3.

[17] *Mundus muliebris*, Transl: *the world of women.* Also, *Immundum muliebrem ptiùs convenìt dìci.* So Tertullian de habitu. mul. cap. 4. Poss. Transl.: *It is more appropriate to call a woman unclean.* Tertullian, On the Apparel of Women, De Habitu Muliebri. Chpt. 2. https://www.newadvent.org/fathers/0402.htm. Accessed April 26, 2025.

should not be the entire world for any of us, as they are with many people who believe that to be out of style, *whatever* that style may currently be, is to exist outside of this world.

Christians are called out of the world and delivered from it. We should display a victory obtained by faith over it![18] It is a prescribed rule of our holy Christian faith, whether they will hear or tolerate it,[19] that "women should adorn themselves in respectable apparel, with modesty and self-control."[20]

Now, there are some who speak out against a vain attitude towards clothing as if it is the worst sin of our day, worse than any other. It is as if they believe this kind of vanity is a new thing and all generations before now did not struggle with the same issue.[21] And others condemn a vain approach to clothing as if their condemnation itself is an extreme opportunity to speak against this vanity.[22] Both these approaches are fully addressed in the excellent sermon of the Church of England entitled, *An Homily against Excess of Apparel,*[23] if the advocates of those positions will only read them. In this message, it is shown that even in the early days of the reformation, this excessive approach to one's style of dress was common throughout the land, and the leaders of the church at the time felt it necessary to address the matter.

However, we should quickly move back to the actual Scripture passage we are addressing.

---

[18] Galatians 1:4; 1 John 5:4.

[19] 1 John 5:4.

[20] 1 Timothy 2:9.

[21] Ecclesiastes 7:10.

[22] SPR Note: This particular sentence was overwhelmingly difficult to rephrase into contemporary English. I believe this wording fits the context and the original, but so you may evaluate on your own, here is the original: *And others on the other hand, condemns it as a piece of phanaticism to witness (as there is occasion) against this vanity.*

[23] https://northamanglican.com/an-homily-against-excess-of-apparel/ Accessed Apr. 26, 2025.

Second, Fall in Love with Better Adornments

Peter attempts to encourage women, and thereby all people, to fall in love with the better adornments. These are adornments of the mind, the graces of the Holy Spirit called the "hidden person of the heart."[24]

Now, Hugo Grotius observes that though Peter is writing to women, he uses a masculine word.[25] He argues then that this is because the adorning the Apostle speaks of is something both men and women should put on. Grace, as a living principle of continual holy thoughts, words, and actions, is sometimes called the new self, [26] sometimes the inner being/self,[27] and in this passage, the *hidden person of the heart.*

This is called a *person* (the hidden *person* of the heart) because it is made up of many parts and members and its works are vital and rational, and it brings the restoration of the dignity of man to these areas, even though, because of sin, all these things were turned into something similar to what the beasts that perish have. This is called the *person of the heart* because out of the heart flows the springs of life.[28] Within the heart lies the springs, the source of the words and actions and therefore into that place is cast the salt of grace, and so all the waters are healed.[29]

---

[24] 1 Peter 3:4.

[25] SPR Note: The word Hugo Grotius is referring to is *Anthropos* which is the word we translate in the ESV as *person*. *Anthropos* is the Greek word for man, and while this can in some cases be a general term (similar to the English word *mankind* which is used to refer to all people including both sexes), this is not always the case. However, this argument fits well here in light of the calling on all of us, certainly not only women, to have a meek and quiet spirit.

[26] Ephesians 4:24.

[27] Romans 7:22 and 2 Corinthians 4:24 respectively.

[28] Proverbs 4:23.

[29] 2 Kings 2:21.

A man is a Christian indeed if he is one inwardly and has both the circumcision and baptism which is of the heart.[30] This is called the *hidden person of the heart* because the work of grace is a secret thing and does not make a big show in the eyes of the world. It is a mystery of godliness,[31] and it is a life that is hidden with Christ in God,[32] the One to whom the secret things belong.[33] Because of this, the saints are called his *hidden ones*[34] for the world does not know them, much less is it visible to anyone of the world what these *hidden ones* will one day become! The King's daughter who is betrothed to Christ is all glorious.[35]

The work of grace in the soul is often represented as a *regeneration* or as being *born again*,[36] and perhaps when this good work is called the *hidden person of the heart*, there may be some allusion to the forming of the bones in the womb of a pregnant woman. This forming of the child in the womb[37] is something Solomon speaks of as inexplicable, similar to that of the way of the Spirit.[38]

Finally, the *hidden person of the heart*, this work of grace in the soul, is formed of that which is incorruptible. It is not something that can become depraved, nor can it be spoiled by the corruption that is in the world through lust. It is "a spring of water" in the soul, "welling up to eternal life."[39]

In this text we are examining, Peter gives an example of one particular grace, one *member* of this *hidden person of the heart*, which everyone of us must adorn ourselves with. This one

---

[30] Romans 2:29.

[31] 1 Timothy 3:16.

[32] Colossians 3:3.

[33] Deuteronomy 29:29.

[34] Psalm 83:3 KJV.

[35] Psalm 45:13.

[36] John 3:3.

[37] Psalm 139:14-16.

[38] Ecclesiastes 11:5. Compare with John 3:8.

[39] John 4:14.

thing is "a gentle and quiet spirit, which in God's sight is very precious."[40]

Observe the following:

The Grace of a Gentle and Quiet Spirit

First, this grace itself, a gentle and quiet spirit, is recommended to us in this passage. This must not only be an outward behaviour of a gentle (meek) and quiet spirit, which is something a man can be forced into, nor is it through some wicked and hidden deception while the soul is rough and turbulent and filled with poison. The words we speak may be "smooth as butter" while war is in the heart,[41] but the word of God is a discerner and judge of the thoughts and intentions of the heart.[42]

The laws set up by our governments may bind a man, forcing him to act properly, but it is only the power of God's grace that will renew a right spirit within him.[43] That is what makes the tree good, and if the tree is good, then the fruit itself will be good.[44]

The God we worship demands our hearts. He looks at who we are and requires truth in our inner being, not only in the duties of our worship to him, those things that should be done in the spirit,[45] but also in the duty we owe to our neighbour—even that must be done with a pure heart and

---

[40] 1 Peter 3:4.
[41] Psalm 55:21.
[42] Hebrews 4:12.
[43] Psalm 51:10.
[44] Matthew 7:17-20.
[45] John 4:24.

without deception! The word of command from the Captain of our salvation is, "guard yourselves in your spirit."[46]

This Grace is Precious

Second, regarding how wonderful this grace is, it is in the sight of God of great price.[47] It is truly a precious form of grace since it is precious in the sight of God—and we know he is unable to deceive or be deceived.

The word used for *precious* in 1 Peter 3:4 and *costly* in 1 Timothy 2:9 is *poluteles*,[48] the same word in each verse, and in 1 Timothy 2:9, it is joined with *gold* and *pearls*.

People who show their quality through the way they adorn themselves do not challenge those who are carefree and content, but those who are rich. They do not make a fancy, impressive show to impress children and fools, but they offer something of intrinsic value, and they commend themselves to the wise.

A meek and quiet spirit is such an adorning. It does not have the carefree attitude that fits with the temperament of a carnal world, but that true worth that entrusts its value to the favour of God. It is one of those graces which are compared to the fragrant powders of a merchant,[49] brought from far away and something of which the merchant, the Lord Jesus Christ, paid dearly for with his precious blood.

From here on, everyone should work hard and be driven in their ambition to, as the greatest honour, whether present or absent, living or dying, we should strive to please the Lord.[50]

---

[46] Malachi 2:15.

[47] 1 Peter 3:4.

[48] SPR Note: This is the word πολυτελής in Greek (Strong's number G4185). The Strong's definition is *extremely expensive: - costly, very precious, of great price*. M. Henry's original included the Greek lettering in this section.

[49] Song of Solomon 3:6.

[50] 2 Corinthians 5:9.

And praise to God, this is something that is attainable through the great mediator, Jesus Christ, from whom we have received a way to walk which pleases him. We must therefore walk with meekness and quietness of spirit, for this, in God's sight, is very precious.

Therefore, a mark of honour is placed in a special way upon the grace of meekness because meekness is commonly despised and looked upon with contempt by the children of this world, a contempt flowing from a meanspirited attitude. However, regardless of how a meek and quiet person is described or treated in this life, they do experience a deep happiness, and this will all be understood soon when God says to those of whom he approves, "Well done, good and faithful servant."[51] For it is by the judgement of Christ that we stand or fall in eternity!

Therefore, here is a way to easily explain this teaching:

Meekness and quietness of spirit is a very wonderful grace which every one of us should put on and adorn ourselves with.

In the course of laying out this teaching in this book, we will endeavour to accomplish the following:

1. To show what this Meekness and Quietness of spirit is.
2. To reveal the wonderful and excellent nature of it.
3. To apply it.

---

[51] Matthew 25:21.

A Discourse on Meekness

I

The Nature of Meekness

Meekness and quietness seem to express the same truth, however the concept of quietness contains a bit of a metaphor in it in the process of illustrating meekness. Because of this, we will speak of these two concepts as though they are distinct, one from another.

We must be of a meek spirit, and this meekness is best understood as a *spirit at ease*. Now, this is not a sinful sort of ease, one which leads to immorality, such as in Ephraim's case as they willingly walked after the commandment of the idolatrous princes.[1] Nor is this a simple ease that allows someone to be pressured and deceived, such as in the case of Rehoboam, who, when he was forty years old, was said to be young and tender-hearted.[2] Instead, this is a gracious ease.

---

[1] Hosea 5:11.
[2] 2 Chronicles 13:7.

That means that which is good and pure will work and affect and shape this ease in a similar way to those whose heart of stone is taken away and are given a heart of flesh![3]

Meekness empowers a soul to endure and accommodate every situation and therefore makes a man at ease with himself and everyone around him. In Latin, a meek man is called *mansuetus,* [4] which alludes to the taming and the reclaiming of wild animals,[5] bringing them to a point where they can be handled and touched. Our corrupt nature has made us like the wild donkey used to the wilderness or like a swift camel travelling along her paths.[6] But when the grace of meekness begins to rule in the soul, it changes the character of the soul in such a way that it can be managed and controlled. "The wolf shall dwell with the lamb, and the leopard shall lie down with the young goat... and a little child shall lead them.... They shall not hurt or destroy in all my holy mountain."[7]

We can consider meekness with respect both *to God* and *to others.*[8] Meekness belongs to both tablets of the law, and has to do with the first great commandment, "You shall love the Lord your God," as well as the second, which is like it, "You shall love your neighbour as yourself."[9] However, meekness points especially to the second.

---

[3] Ezekiel 36:26-27.

[4] *Mansuetus: qu. manu assuetus; us'd to the hand.* SPR Note: This Latin phrase followed by the English translation essentially points to a concept of an animal trained *by the hand* to be gentle or tame. For believers, we are to be *tamed* by the hand of the Spirit to be gentle.

[5] James 3:7-8.

[6] Jeremiah 2:23-24.

[7] Isaiah 11:6, 9.

[8] SPR Note: The original says *to our brethren* here, which in a Christian context feels like it refers to fellow believers, but Henry appears to apply this to everyone (believers and unbelievers alike). As such, I have used the word *others* instead of *brethren.*

[9] Deuteronomy 6:5; Leviticus 19:18.

1. Meekness towards God

When we speak of meekness towards God, we need to understand it as the easy and quiet submission of the soul to his entire will, as much as he is pleased to reveal to us, whether by his word or by his providence.[10]

Meekness towards God is the silent submission of the soul to the word of God. Meekness is the bowing of our understanding to every divine truth and submitting our will to every divine command and doing both without grumbling or arguing. The word then becomes an "implanted word,"[11] when it is received with meekness, that is, when we receive it with a sincere willingness to be taught and a desire to learn.

  a. Meekness is a grace that cuts open the stem and holds it open, so that the Wjord, as another sprout, may be grafted in.
  b. Meekness breaks up the fallow ground[12] and prepares it for the seed to be planted.
  c. Meekness captivates the deep thoughts and lays the soul out before God's pen like a sheet of white paper.

When the dawn arrives and takes hold on the earth, it is said to be changed like clay under the seal.[13] Similar to this, meekness prepares the soul to receive the rays of God's light, even though the soul has, in the past, rebelled against that light. It also opens the heart, as Lydia's was opened, and sets us down with Mary at the feet of Christ, the learner's place and posture.[14]

For the meek, there is a promise of teaching—they will be taught because they are predisposed to learn. "He... teaches

---

[10] SPR Note: *Providence* would refer to God's guidance or care, and perhaps also his power in guiding human destiny.

[11] James 1:21.

[12] SPR Note: Unused and unprepared soil.

[13] Job 38:12-14.

[14] Luke 10:38-42; Acts 16:14.

the [meek] his way."[15] The word of God is good news, he "brings good news to the [meek]"[16] and they will receive and welcome it into their lives. The poor in spirit have good news preached to them,[17] and the gift of Wisdom is given to those who daily wait with meekness at her gates,[18] who, like beggars, wait at wisdom's door posts.[19]

Meekness towards God is the silent submission of the soul to the word of God.

The language of meekness is spoken by many:

a. It is spoken by Samuel as a child when he says, "Speak, Lord, for your servant hears."[20]

b. It is spoken by Joshua who, when he was appointed to such a high position commanding all of Israel and defying all their enemies—filled with great and bold thoughts—even so, when he received a command from heaven, he submitted himself to it asking, "What does my Lord say to his servant?"[21]

c. It is spoken by the Apostle Paul in his first breath as a new man when he asks, "What shall I do, Lord?"[22]

---

[15] Psalm 25:8-9.

[16] Isaiah 61:1.

[17] Matthew 11:5.

[18] Proverbs 8:1-5.

[19] Proverbs 8:34.

[20] 1 Samuel 3:9.

[21] Joshua 5:14.

[22] Acts 22:10 SPR Note: The original reference in M. Henry's book points back to Acts 9:6, but that verse refers to a command from Jesus rather than a question as in Acts 22. As such, I have changed this reference to accommodate this detail.

d. It is spoken by Cornelius when he says, "We are all here in the presence of God to hear all that you have been commanded by the Lord."[23]

e. It is spoken by the good man I have read of whom, when he was going to hear the word, used to say, "Now let the word of the Lord come; and if I had six hundred necks, I would bow them all to the authority of it."[24]

To receive the word with meekness is to step into it as if you were to step into a mould. This appears to be Paul's metaphor in Romans 6:17 when he refers to becoming "obedient from the heart to the standard of teaching to which you were committed."

Meekness softens the wax, so that it may receive the impression of the seal, whether it is for doctrine or reproof, for correction or instruction in righteousness.[25] It opens the ear to discipline, silences our objections, and suppresses the unspiritual and fleshly mind when it rises against the Word.[26] Meekness leads us to agree that the law is good[27] and to consider all the commandments about all things to be right, even when they place restraints on us.

---

[23] Acts 10:33.

[24] SPR Note: This quote is often attributed to Johannes Œcolampadius.

[25] 2 Timothy 3:16-17.

[26]*Mitescere est non contradicere divinae Scripturae sive intellectae si vitiae percutit, sive non intellectae quasi nos melius sapere possemus.* Aug. l. 2. de doctrina Christi. Transl. *To be meek is not to contradict Holy Writ, whether we understand it, if it condemn our evil ways, or understand it not, as though we might know better and have a clearer insight of the truth.* Augustine, SUMMA THEOLOGIAE: Clemency and meekness (Secunda Secundae Partis, Q. 157). (2023). https://www.newadvent.org/summa/3157.htm. Accessed Sept. 4, 2025.

[27] *ilecere esd non contradicere divina Scripture sive inlellecte, si vitis percutil, sivenon intollecte, queri nos melius sapere possemus. True meekness will prevent us from opposing either the obvious parts of Scripture, severely as they may task our vices, or the mysterious parts, in reading which vanity may suggest that we could have dictated what is more profitable.* Augustine, On Christian Doctrine, Book II, Section 9. https://www.newadvent.org/fathers/12022.htm. Accessed June 4, 2025.

Meekness is the silent submission of the soul to *the providence of God,* for that is also God's will for us.

Meekness is the silent submission of the soul to the providence of God, for that is also God's will for us.

a. When God's Work Is Difficult and Painful

When God's work[28] in the world and in our lives is difficult and painful, it upsets us and shakes up our plans and desires for our lives. In those times, meekness not only quiets our hearts, but brings us into peace with what God is doing. Meekness enables us to endure, and to accept evil as well as good from the hand of the Lord.

This is the wonderful position that Job reasons himself into.[29] This meek posture leads us to kiss the rod[30] and even to accept the punishment of our sinful ways, accepting everything God does as good. It is to not dare to fight with our Maker,

---

[28] SPR Note: Original uses the word, *providence.*

[29] Job. 2:10.

[30] Samuel Rutherford, Joshua redivivus, 1664, …*pass by your daughter and kiss the Lord's rod.* p. 427. https://quod.lib.umich.edu/e/eebo/A57970.0001.001. Accessed Aug. 29, 2025. This could also be a reference to Samuel Butler's poem entitled, Hudibras, 1660-1680, line 840. https://www.exclassics.com/hudibras/hudibras.pdf. Accessed Aug. 29, 2025. SPR Note: Consider the *rod* to be the rod of punishment or discipline.

nor set out to tell God what he should do.[31] Instead, meekness leads us to hold our tongue, even to the point of leaving ourselves incapable of speech, simply because God is the one doing this work.[32]

How meek was Aaron when God's wrath was poured out, resulting in the loss of his sons' lives. In that moment, "Aaron held his peace."[33] Aaron found himself satisfied in the act of God's sanctification and because of that satisfaction, he had nothing to say against the work of God.

David, however, showed the opposite of Aaron's meekness. Although he was considered a man after God's own heart earlier in his life, when it came to the matter of Uzzah, David's anger showed him not to be a man after God's own heart. On that day, he was upset at God when he killed Uzzah[34] as if God was supposed to ask David's permission to protect the honour of the ark of the covenant. When God's anger is kindled, our anger must be suppressed.

This is the law of meekness that whatever pleases God must not displease us.

David was in a better mindset when he wrote the 56th Psalm, the title of which some believe speaks of the calmness and submissiveness of his spirit when the Philistines took him in Gath. It is entitled, *The Silent Dove Afar Off.*

What was far off? The danger he faced! So he was then as a silent dove. Perhaps he was mourning,[35] but he was not complaining, nor was he struggling, nor did he resist when he

---

[31] SPR Note: The original uses the phrase, *nor desiring to prescribe to him* which appears to mean *not desiring to lay out a command or rule to God beforehand.* The phrasing used above appears to encapsulate that concept.

[32] SPR Note: Notice how countercultural this concept is. In a world where we value and prize *speaking up* and *speaking our minds*, meekness calls us to hold our tongue and accept our fate simply because God is the one sitting in the driver's seat!

[33] Leviticus 10:3.

[34] 2 Samuel 6:8.

[35] Isaiah 38:14.

was seized by the birds of prey. The psalm he penned in this time was a Michtam,[36] a golden psalm.

This is the law of meekness that whatever pleases God must not displease us.

This language of meekness is spoken by Eli when he said, "It is the Lord,"[37] and by David in the same way, "Here I am, let him do to me what seems good to him."[38]

The heart of meekness accepts God's movement and work in this world:

a. Not only that God *can* do what he desires, pointing to his power as there is no one who can hold him back.

b. Not only that God *may* do what he desires, pointing to his sovereignty, because God does not need to give account for anything he does.

c. Not only that God *will* do what he desires, pointing to his unchangeableness, because God knows what he thinks, and no one can change his mind.

But, the heart of meekness declares, "*Let him do* what he desires," pointing to his wisdom and goodness as Hezekiah did when he said, "The word of the Lord that you have spoken is good."[39] Let God do what he desires because he will do what is best! Because of this, if God was to hand the decision to us—if we have meek and quiet souls, confident that God knows what is good for us more than we do for ourselves—

---

[36] *Michtam* is a term used for Psalms 16 and 56-60. It is uncertain what this term means, but these Psalms are often called *Golden Psalms*.

[37] 1 Samuel 3:18.

[38] 2 Samuel 15:25-26.

[39] Isaiah 39:8.

we would hand it back to him saying, "Let God choose our inheritance for us!"[40]

b. When God's Work Is Dark and Intricate

When God's work in our lives and in this world is *dark and intricate,* and we are quite at a loss as to what God is about to do with us—his way is in the sea, and his path in the great waters, and his footsteps are not known,[41] clouds and darkness are round about him[42]—a meek and quiet spirit confidently accepts that all things will work together for good for us, if we love God,[43] even though we cannot comprehend how.

A quiet and meek spirit teaches us to follow God with a deeply rooted faith[44] as Abraham did when he followed the Lord's call, not knowing *where* he was going, but knowing very well *who* he followed.[45] Meekness quiets our hearts so that though we don't know what our Lord is doing now, we trust that we will know later.[46] When poor Job faced such terrible suffering, he couldn't trace the footsteps of God's work throughout his horrific situation and was almost lost in the labyrinth of his pain,[47] even so, how quietly he sits down with

---

[40] Psalm 47:4.

[41] Psalm 77:19.

[42] Psalm 97:2.

[43] Romans 8:28.

[44] SPR Note: The original uses the phrase *implicit faith* here which appears to point to a faith that is interwoven throughout our hearts and lives. Perhaps a solid understanding here might be a *life that is well saturated with a deeply rooted faith, interwoven throughout our hearts and minds,* however, that might be a tad wordy.

[45] Hebrews 11:8.

[46] John 13:7.

[47] Job 23:8-9.

this thought, "But he knows the way that I take; when he has tried me, I shall come out as gold."[48]

2. Meekness towards Others

There is a meekness that can be shown towards others and towards "all people."[49]

Meekness has a particular influence on the affliction of too much anger. It does not, however, seek to fully destroy[50] or exterminate a proper holy indignation from out of the soul, something of which Scripture speaks.[51] To do such a thing would be to extinguish a burning coal that is sometimes necessary, even before the altar of God, and to blunt the edge of the spiritual weapons which we are to carry on our spiritual warfare. Instead, the task of meekness is to direct and govern this affliction of anger that we may be angry and not sin.[52]

Now, considering meekness in both a philosophical and Christian sense, we learn the following. Meekness, in a philosophical sense, is a virtue that exists separate from two extremes. On one hand, it is far from the extreme of rash, excessive anger; and on the other hand, it is far from the extreme of a total lack of anger. This is a position of which Aristotle confessed was very difficult to attain.[53]

---

[48] Job 23:10.

[49] Titus 3:2.

[50] *Not* απαθεια - *insensibility, but* μετριοπαθεια - *moderation. Anger is coe fortidudinis. The whetstone of courage.*

[51] Original: *Meekness is especially conversant about the affection of anger, not wholly to extirpate and eradicate it out of the soul…*

[52] Ephesians 4:26.

[53] Aristotle, Nicomachean Ethics, Book IV, chapt. 5. https://classics.mit.edu/Aristotle/nicomachaen.4.iv.html. Accessed June 4, 2025.

Meekness, in a Christian sense, is one of the fruits of the Spirit.[54] It is a grace[55] brought about by the Holy Spirit both as something which sanctifies us and as a comfort in the hearts of all true believers. This grace of meekness is something that teaches and enables us at all times to keep our passions under the control[56] and rule of the Christian faith[57] and proper reason.

I have observed that this fruit of meekness is produced in the hearts of all true believers, because, even though there are some believers whose natural temperament is sour or harsh, wherever there is true grace, there is a desire to strive against that harshness. And in this working of the Holy Spirit, there is given some measure of strength to overcome that sour disposition. However, just as with other graces given to us, an absolute sinless perfection cannot be attained in this life. Even so, we are to work hard for it and to press on in that direction.

To be more specific, the work and responsibility of meekness is to enable us to wisely control our own anger whenever we are provoked and to patiently endure the anger of others, not allowing ourselves to be provoked. The former here is the responsibility primarily of those in positions of authority, the latter is the responsibility of those under

---

[54] Galatians 5:22-23.

[55] *both gratis data, and gratum faciens.* SPR Note: *Gratis data* refers to gifts given for the benefit of others (such as spiritual gifts), and *gratum faciens* would refer to a sanctifying grace. These theological terms tends to be used more within Catholic and Eastern Orthodox churches than within Protestant denominations.

[56] SPR Note: In the original, the word here is *conduct* which, in an older sense, carried the concept of *leading* or *guiding*, therefore *control* is used for this sentence as it appears to convey the concept.

[57] SPR Note: In the original, the word *religion* is used here. In contemporary times, Christians have drawn a distinction between *religion* and *faith*, considering the former to be works-based and the latter to be indicative of true religion. While this distinction can be helpful at times, it is not entirely an accurate understanding of these words. However, due to this contemporary perspective, I will often change the word *religion* to *faith* or *Christian faith* so as to accommodate this current viewpoint.

authority, and both are the responsibilities of those in equal positions.

Meekness teaches us to prudently govern our own anger whenever something occurs that might provoke us. Just as the quality of temperance helps us to moderate our natural appetites in the things that are desirable to us, the quality of meekness helps us to moderate our natural passions against those things that upset us, helping to guide and control our resentments.

Anger in the soul is like a frisky horse: it is good if it is well managed. Continuing with this metaphor, meekness is then the horse's bridle. Wisdom is the hand that sets the boundaries for our anger, forces it to act properly, and keeps it in check in an even, steady, and regular pace. Meekness reduces the anger when it turns aside from the path, just as the bridle keeps the horse on the straight and narrow. Meekness preserves our behaviour, keeping it proper and true, and restraining our anger and pulling it back whenever it grows headstrong and outrageous, and threatens to bring trouble to ourselves or others.[58]

Anger must then be held in, just like the horse and mule with the bit and bridle,[59] so that it does not break through the boundaries and run down everyone who stands in its way or even throw the rider himself headlong.

---

[58] SPR Note: this particular section in the original was quite difficult to rewrite into modern English as M. Henry jumps around in his metaphor so much that it is difficult to identify at times if he is speaking in metaphor regarding the horse and bridle or direct in terms of meekness holding back anger. As such, I have attempted to work through this by emphasizing the direct teaching of meekness and anger while using the metaphor as a support for the concept.

[59] Psalm 32:9.

What we say about fire is true of anger:[60] it is a good servant but a bad master. It is good in the fireplace, but bad on the curtains.

Meekness keeps that anger in its place, setting boundaries to the sea and declares, "Thus far shall you come, and no farther, and here shall your proud waves be stayed."[61]

In regard to our own anger, whenever we find it rising in our souls, the task of meekness is to do the following four things:

a. To consider the circumstances
b. To calm the spirit
c. To curb the tongue
d. To cool the heat of passion

a. Meekness Considers the Circumstances

The work of meekness in our hearts is to bring us to a point where we *consider the circumstances* surrounding the situation in which we feel provoked to anger. We should never express our displeasure without *first* taking the time for proper, mature consideration.

The work of meekness is to keep reason on the throne in the soul as it should be, keeping our thinking clear and uncloudy, and our judgment untainted and unbiased in the midst of the most provoking experiences. This will allow us to see everything properly in its true light, seeing it in its own colour, and to make decisions accordingly. This work of meekness enables us to maintain "silence in the court," so that the still small voice in which the Lord resides, as he did with

---

[60] *Non cognoscilur audacia nisi in bello, amicus nisi in aecessisele, sapiens nisi in ira. It is in war, that we discover the hero; in a time of need, the friend; and during anger, the man of wisdom.* Arab proverb.

[61] Job 38:11.

A Discourse on Meekness

Elijah at Mount Horeb,[62] may not be drowned out by the noisy storms of our passions.

A meek man, therefore, will never be angry at a child, a servant, or a friend unless he has first seriously weighed the matter in just and even balances, while a steady and impartial hand holds the scales, and a free and unprejudiced thought judges the anger necessary.

It is said of our Lord Jesus in John 11:33 that he troubled himself which suggests it was an intentional emotion, something for which he saw reason and therefore made the choice to feel the emotion.[63]

Things go right in the soul when we hold no affection for any resentment unless we have first put it through the scrutiny of our reason and understanding and then, and only then, allow it entrance into our thinking. The emotions of anger and resentment that do not come in through this door of reason but climb up and over the wall some other way are the same as thieves and robbers, and we must always be on guard against them!

In a time of war—and truthfully, every sanctified soul is in a constant war between grace and corruption—care must be taken to examine all travellers in and out of a country, especially those who approach carrying weapons. These potential enemies must be examined to determine where they

---

[62] 1 Kings 19:12-13.

[63] ἰτάραξε ἑαυτὸ - *he troubled himself.* SPR Note: The KJV and ESV translate this as passive (Jesus was troubled) as though *the troubling* happened to him rather than *he troubled himself.* Now, my Greek is far from what it used to be, however, let me attempt to draw upon a capacity once held for just a moment. The Greek verb is aorist (undefined) active suggesting a simple, snapshot of an action accomplished by the subject (*he troubled*), and it is immediately followed by the pronoun εαυτον (*himself*). This word (εαυτον) is a reflexive pronoun which points out that the subject (*Jesus*) is not only the actor of the verb, but also the receiver of the action (*he troubled himself*). So, the original Greek wording of this verse does, in fact, as M. Henry points out, suggest that Jesus took the action to trouble himself. M. Henry applied this concept well!

come from, where they are travelling to, who they stand for, and what they want. And just as this is the case for a nation in a time of war, so it should also be in the well-disciplined soul.

Let meekness stand as a guard, a sentinel in your life, so that when something approaches that might provoke you, you can examine who you are about to be angry with[64] and if there is a valid reason. In this process, ask the following questions:

a. What are the details of this offense?
b. What is the actual offence?
c. What was the nature of the offense and how did it come about?
d. What is the consequence of any resentment we might have?
e. What harm will come if we hold down our resentments, refusing to allow them freedom to boil?

Every sanctified soul is in a constant war between grace and corruption.

Meekness will bring forward questions such as these to the soul, and as meekness determines the answer to these questions, we will then understand all that our anger is trying to push us to do. Meekness only listens to reason in the matter, just as every rational person.

In James, we find three great statements of meekness all in one Scripture. "Let every person be quick to hear, slow to

---

[64] *Expendantur verba, dicendum hoc, si dicen dum adversum hunc, tempus sermonis sit hujus, &c.* Transl. *and weighing his words — as to whether this should be said, that should be answered, or whether it be a suitable time for this remark.* Ambr. de Offic. l. 1. c. 9. Ambrose's On the Duties of the Clergy, chapt. 4. https://www.newadvent.org/fathers/34011.htm. Accessed June 5, 2025.

speak, slow to anger." [65] Some believe that these three statements are hidden in the three proper names of Ishmael's sons,[66] (which in the beginning of the wars, Bishop Prideaux spoke of to a man who had been his student, sharing his thoughts as the summary of his advice) *Mishma, Dumah,* and *Massa.* The meanings of these names are *hear, keep silence,* and *bear.* Hear reason and keep passion silent, then you will not find it difficult to bear up under a provoking experience.

It is said of the Holy One of Israel, when the Egyptians provoked him, that he weighed a path for his anger.[67] Justice first weighed the cause in the scales and then anger poured out the judgement.[68]

In this way, the Lord came down to see the pride of the builders of the tower of Babel[69] before he scattered them and to see the wickedness of Sodom[70] before he overthrew it, though in both cases their sin was obvious and barefaced.[71] This teaches us to think before we grow angry, and to judge before we pass sentence, so that in this matter we might be true followers of God, his dear children, and be merciful as our Father in heaven is merciful.

In James, we read of the "meekness of wisdom,"[72] for if that wisdom, the wisdom that helps show us the proper path

---

[65] James 1:19.

[66] Genesis 25:14; 1 Chronicles 1:30.

[67] Psalm 78:50. SPR NOTE: The Hebrew פָלַס (translated "made" in both KJV and ESV) can mean to mentally weigh an issue or to ponder. Also, M. Henry includes the phrase here, *so the margin reads it from the Hebrew.*

[68] *Libravit semitam irae suae.* SPR Note: The original uses the word, *vials* in place of *judgement.*

[69] Genesis 11:5.

[70] Genesis 18:21.

[71] *In corrept one vitiorum subesse menti debet Iracundia, non praeesse.* Transl. *In reproving vice, though we admit a degree of anger, we should not suffer it to usurp arbitrary sway.* Gregory the Great, Moralia. https://www.lectionarycentral.com/GregoryMoralia/ Accessed June 4, 2025.

[72] James 3:13.

and the wisdom of the prudent man who can discern his way,[73] if all that wisdom is lacking, meekness will not remain in the heart. It is our rash reactions and our lack of careful reflection on the matter at hand that hands us over to all the trouble brought on by uncontrolled anger. We then, in our rashness, hand the reins of our lives over to that anger, the very reins that should be kept in the hands of reason, and our anger drives us quickly over a thousand cliffs.

When anger demands immediate judgement of a matter, meekness calls for more time.

The book of Nehemiah offers an excellent example of wisdom at work in righteous anger. Nehemiah declares, "I was very angry when I heard their outcry,"[74] but that anger did not at all break the laws of meekness, for he said, "I took counsel with myself," or as the Hebrew puts it, "My heart consulted in me." Before he went out and told them how angry he was, he reflected in his own heart and took time to think soberly on the matter. Once this was accomplished, he rebuked the nobles in a very solid, rational conversation, and the result was good![75]

---

[73] Ecclesiastes 10:10; Proverbs 14:8; *Ratio id judicare vult quod aequum videri vult est, Ira id aequum videri vult, quod judicavit.* Transl. *Reason prompts us to pass a righteous judgment; anger first hurries us into an opinion, and then, whatever it is, resolves to maintain it.* Seneca, On Anger, Book I, chapt. XXII. https://standardebooks.org/ebooks/seneca/dialogues/aubrey-stewart/text/on-anger. Accessed June 4, 2025.

[74] Nehemiah 5:6-7.

[75] Nehemiah 5:8-13.

In every situation when anger demands immediate judgement of a matter, meekness calls for more time to work through the issue fairly and to accept counsel from both sides.

When the offended Levite reacted in such a barbaric manner, hoping to anger the tribes of Israel[76] against the men of Gibeah, even so the people, once they received that horrific announcement, referred the matter to their consideration. This teaches us to do the same when, in our hearts, we are considering revenge.[77] And so, the counsel for us is to consider it, take advice, and then speak our mind.[78]

Whenever Job had an argument with his servants, he called for a rational discussion of the matter and to hear what they had to say for themselves. He says, "What then shall I do when God rises up?" and "Did not he who made me in the womb make him?"[79]

When our hearts are hot within us, we would do well to ask ourselves the same question that God asked Cain. "Why am I angry?"[80] And perhaps this question will lead to others like it.

a. Why am I angry at all?
b. Why have I grown angry so quickly?
c. Why so very angry?
d. Why have I been so moved by this and lost so much control over myself by my anger?
e. What rational reason is there for my anger?
f. Do I do well to be angry for a plant that came up in a night and perished in a night?[81]
g. Should I be so deeply hurt by such a sudden and temporary hurt?

---

[76] *Who were typically so easily worked up that they did not need much help in this area.*

[77] Judges 19:30.

[78] SPR Note: Not all original versions include this paragraph.

[79] Job 31:13-15.

[80] Genesis 4:6.

[81] Jonah 4:9.

h. Will not a cooler head at a later time quickly clear up these growing resentments, and therefore, would it not be better to rein them in now?

These are questions, the rational considerations, a person asks when they live within the meekness of wisdom.

b. Meekness Calms the Spirit

The work of meekness is also to *calm the spirit*, so that the inward peace you have is not disturbed by any outward attack.

There is no doubt that we can express our displeasure at the wrong actions of others whenever there is a need to do so, but this can be done without allowing resentment to boil up inside and throw our own souls into a rage.

What benefit is there if we tear ourselves[82] in our anger?[83] Is it not possible to mount a charge against the enemy without throwing our own troops into disarray? Certainly we can, if meekness rules in our hearts! This rule is a grace which helps to keep a man as master of himself while he fights to master another, and it protects the heart against outward attacks. When we are protected like this by meekness, the attacks that come will not harm us much, nor will they rob us of the peace in our hearts or disturb the rest we feel in our souls.

Just as we are called to show patience in times of suffering, so also meekness is the call on our hearts during times of anger as it allows us to maintain control of our soul. This is shown in Luke 21:19 in the hopes that we will not lose what we have.

In Christ's farewell sermon to his disciples, we find the emphasis jumps right out at us in his first words: "Let not your hearts be troubled."[84] It is the responsibility of and a benefit to all faithful people to not allow trouble to enter their hearts, to

---

[82] SPR Note: Or *soul* as in the Hebrew of Job 18:4.

[83] Job 18:4.

[84] John 14:1.

keep their hearts even and calm, even though, as Job declares, the eye continues to see the provocation of this world.[85]

"The wicked[86] are like the tossing sea; for it cannot be quiet," [87] but the peace of God which surpasses all understanding guards the hearts and minds[88] of all the meek of the earth. Meekness protects the mind from being ruffled and agitated, and the spirit from falling apart due to all the temptations and the provocations of this lower world. Meekness stills the noise of the sea, the crashing of her waves, and the upheaval of the soul. It does not allow angry passions to tear us apart like confused, rampaging people, but meekness faces each emotion one at a time, ready to march, charge, fire, or retreat as wisdom and grace direct.

It is said of the just and holy God that he is the Lord of his anger.[89] We translate it wrathful (which is perhaps not a good translation as wrath is not in him[90]), but he is Lord and master of anger,[91] *Compos irae,*[92] and we should work to be like him in this. Some interpreters believe this is the meaning of what God said to Cain, "Its desire is contrary to you, but you must rule over it,"[93] over this passionate anger which has come from deep within. Cain needed to do this, and if he used the grace offered to him, he could have subdued and held down his unrestrained anger, so that it would not upset the peace in his soul or lead him into sin.[94]

---

[85] Job 17:2.

[86] *The turbulent and unquiet, as the world primarily signifies.*

[87] Isaiah 57:20.

[88] Philippians 4:7.

[89] Nahum 1:2.

[90] Isaiah 27:4.

[91] חמה בעל *the Lord of anger.*

[92] Translation: *I control my anger.*

[93] Genesis 4:7.

[94] SPR Note: Not all original versions include this paragraph.

c. Meekness Curbs the Tongue

Meekness will *curb the tongue,* and "guard the mouth as with a muzzle" when the heart is "hot."[95] Even when there is a need for harsh words and we are called to rebuke sharply, [96] meekness forbids all wrath and indecent language, everything that sounds like clamor or malice.[97] In fact, we see that Moses set aside his meekness when he spoke that foolish word, "rebels," that kept him from entering Canaan, even though the people truly were rebellious, inciting anger.[98]

Men in the midst of deep anger are more likely to speak abusively and to call names, even to take the blessed name of God in vain and so profane it. It is a disgusting way by which the children of hell vent their anger by swearing at those in their employ, other people, even their animals, or anything that upsets them. When men are in the midst of this deep anger, they are likely to reveal secrets, make foolish vows and resolutions (which later turn out to trip them up), sometimes to slander and lie about their brothers, bring forward angry accusations, do the devil's work, and to speak without thought concerning others,[99] things of which they later see need to repent.

When Saul called his own son, the heir to the throne, the "son of a perverse, rebellious woman,"[100] he spoke foolishly.[101] In the filthy dialect of our days, this phrase would mean "son of a whore," which is a fine credit to himself and his family![102]

---

[95] Psalm 39:1-3.

[96] ἀποτόμως - *cuttingly.* Titus 1:13.

[97] Ephesians 4:31.

[98] Numbers 20:10.

[99] Original, *speak that in their haste.* Psalm 116:11.

[100] 1 Samuel 20:30.

[101] SPR Note: Perhaps a better word here might be *stupidly* as the original uses the word *brutishly.*

[102] SPR Note: Not all original versions include this sentence.

A Discourse on Meekness

"Racca" and "You fool!" are declared by our Saviour as breaking the law of the sixth commandment,[103] and anger in the heart is no excuse for such disgraceful words.[104] Instead, that anger is the very thing that makes these words so malicious! These vicious words are the smoke from the fire of that anger and the gall and wormwood springing from the root of bitterness.[105] And if for "every careless word they speak"[106] they will give an account, so much more for wicked words like these!

And just as murder is an insult to God's sovereignty, so it is similar when we curse men who are made in God's image,[107] as if they are inferior to us, that is, speaking evil of them or wishing evil upon them. This is the disease which meekness prevents![108]

Meekness, then, functions as a law of kindness for the tongue.[109] It is to the tongue as the helm is to the ship,[110] not for the purpose of silencing it, but to guide and to steer it wisely, especially when the wind is heavy.[111]

If at any time we have allowed anger and evil thoughts to invade our hearts, meekness will place a hand over our mouths

---

[103] Matthew 5:22.

[104] *As is often the excuse.*

[105] Hebrews 12:15.

[106] Matthew 12:36.

[107] James 3:9.

[108] SPR Note: In the original, this statement is a compound sentence with the first sentence of the next paragraph, which made little sense to little old me.

[109] Proverbs 31:26.

[110] James 3:3-4.

[111] *In Sorate irae signum erat, vocem submittere, loqui parcius apparebat tunc illum sibi obstare.* Transl. *Anger was indicated in Socrates by his speaking little, and in a low key; thus he was observed to maintain a conflict within himself.* Seneca, On Anger, Book I, chapt. XIII, https://standardebooks.org/ebooks/seneca/dialogues/aubrey-stewart/text/on-anger . Accessed June 4, 2025. Plutarch *de non irascendo*. Plutarch, On Not Being Angry. https://www.perseus.tufts.edu/hopper/text?doc=Perseus%3Atext%3A2008.01.0263%3Asection%3D4. Accessed April 1, 2025.

22

(following the wise man's advice[112]) to keep that evil thought from venting through any wicked words that might reflect poorly upon God or our brother. Meekness will argue a point without yelling, give instruction without insult, convince a man of his foolishness without calling him a fool, teach those in positions of authority not to threaten (or as it reads in the margin to moderate it),[113] and will reflect deeply on the matter lest any root of bitterness spring up, causing trouble, and through it defile us and others.[114]

d. Meekness Cools the Heat of Passion

First, meekness will *cool the heat of angry passions* quickly and not allow it to continue. Just as meekness keeps us from quickly growing angry, it also teaches us when we are angry to calm down quickly. A meek man's anger is like a spark from flint and steel—it's difficult to get the spark, but when it does come, it quickly goes out.[115]

The wisdom from above is gentle and therefore not likely to provoke others, so it is easy to be negotiated with when anything upsetting arises, always ready to hear the first offer and proposal of amends, submission, and reconciliation.[116] And when this happens, anger is turned away!

The one who is meek will be quick to forgive injuries and confrontations and will always have some excuse or word ready to downplay the insult or brush it off, while an angry man, for the purpose of inflating and justifying his resentment, will diligently aggravate the offense.

---

[112] Proverbs 30:32.

[113] Ephesians 6:9.

[114] Hebrews 12:15.

[115] Original: *The anger of a meek man is like fire struck out of steel—hard to be got out; and when it is, soon gone.*

[116] James 3:17.

The meek response is to say, "No harm done,[117] or if there was, it wasn't intentional, maybe it was just an oversight." When the offense is looked at through this kind of lens, downplaying the harm, it is then easy to ignore it, and the anger quickly fades. The fire is quenched before it takes control, and by a quick intervention, the plague is stopped.

The world is so full of the sparks of insult, and there is so much tinder in the hearts of even the best of us, that it is no wonder that anger sometimes *enters* the heart of a wise man. However, it *abides* only in the heart of a fool.[118]

Angry thoughts, just like other worthless thoughts, may rush into the heart suddenly, surprising us with their arrival, but meekness will never allow those thoughts to lodge there,[119] nor will it allow the sun to go down on that anger.[120] For if the heart does allow it to remain, there is danger that the anger will rise bloody the next morning!

Anger allowed to boil turns into malice. The wisdom of meekness, by properly applying itself, disperses the angry mood or state of mind before it comes to a head.

One would have thought that when David was so enraged at Nabal's abuse that nothing short of the blood of Nabal and all his house could quench David's rage, but it was satisfied by far less. He showed meekness by yielding to the diversion offered by Abigail's present and speech, and he did this with satisfaction and thankfulness. He was not only quickly

---

[117] *Tis a Maxim in the Law, In verbis dubiis benignior sententia est praeferenda. And semper fit praesumptio in meliorem partem.* Transl. *On words of dubious import we should pass a favourable construction. And, Somper fii præsumplio in meliorem partem. We should always presume on the candid side.* Andrea Alciato, De Praesumptionibus (On Presumptions). SPR Note: I apologize. I could not find a proper link.

[118] Ecclesiastes 7:9.

[119] Jeremiah 4:14.

[120] Ephesians 4:26.

pacified, but he also blessed her and blessed God for Abigail having pacified him.[121]

God does not argue forever, nor is he always full of wrath, "for his anger is but for a moment."[122] How unlike him are those whose sword devours forever and whose anger burns like the coals of a juniper![123] But the grace of meekness, if it fails to keep the soul's peace from being broken, even so, it will not fail to recover that peace immediately and fix the issue. And when the smallest overwhelming emotion arises, meekness brings help in time of need, restores the soul, puts it back together again, and leaves the situation in such a state that no harm has been done.

This is what meekness accomplishes in the rule of our anger.

Second, meekness teaches and enables us to patiently *endure the anger of others*. This quality of meekness applies especially when dealing with employers and fellow employees.[124] Just as fire kindles fire, often what provokes anger is other anger. Meekness prevents that violent collision which forces out these sparks, and it softens at least one side of the conflict. This puts a stop to a great deal of arguments because it's not the first blow that makes a fight, but the second.

Our first goal should be to prevent the anger of others by giving no offense to anyone, but becoming all things to all men, everyone striving to please his neighbour for the good of edification.[125] We should endeavour, as much as it depends on us, to accommodate the emotional needs of all those we interact with and to act in an acceptable and agreeable manner towards them. How much better would our relationships with

---

[121] 1 Samuel 25.

[122] Psalm 30:5.

[123] SPR Note: Juniper wood is known for burning hot and long and for producing hot coals that last.

[124] Original: *superiors and equals*.

[125] Romans 15:2; 1 Corinthians 9:20-23.

others be if all our conversations and interactions with them made use of this art of accommodating?

The tribe of Naphtali was famous for speaking fine words[126] and was satisfied with favour, full of the blessing of the Lord[127] for "whoever gives an honest answer kisses the lips."[128]

In marriage, it is taken for granted that the husband is to care for his wife by pleasing her, and the care of the wife is to please her husband.[129] Where there is that mutual care for one another, there will be no lack of enjoyment.

There is so much tinder in the hearts of even the best of us, that it is no wonder that anger sometimes *enters* the heart of a wise man. However, it *abides* only in the heart of a fool.

There are those who love to be unkind and take pleasure in hurting others, those who put effort into provoking people they find emotional and easy to upset. They are trying to get them "drunk" so that they can look upon their shame,[130] because when those they target grow angry, they end up exposing themselves. In this, they make a mockery of sin and

---

[126] Genesis 49:21 KJV.
[127] Deuteronomy 33:23.
[128] Proverbs 24:26.
[129] 1 Corinthians 7:33-34.
[130] Habakuk 2:15-16.

become like a madman who throws burning embers, arrows, and death, then simply says, "I'm just playing around!"

However, the law of Christ forbids us to provoke one another,[131] except when it comes to provoking one another "to love and good works."[132] That law of Christ instead commands us to "bear one another's burdens and so fulfil the law of Christ."[133]

When Others Are Angry

Now that we understand that we will have to put great effort[134] into the work of keeping everyone pleased[135] and that we will have to suffer greatly[136] at times in order to avoid giving offense, we must now shift our focus to how we should behave when others around us are angry, so that we won't take things from bad to worse.

This is one principle in which those who are younger are called to submit themselves to those who are older[137]—no, in which *all of us* must be subject to one another.[138] In this area, meekness is of use, either *to call for silence* or *to give a soft answer.*[139]

---

[131] Galatians 5:26.

[132] Hebrews 10:24.

[133] Galatians 6:2.

[134] SPR Note: The original here states, *to rise betimes* which refers to rising early. In this context, it appears to ultimately speak of the task of work and effort.

[135] SPR Note: Perhaps in our context, it is helpful to consider something here. I would suggest there is a difference between a meek person's attempt to please others out of love for them and for peace as opposed to what we, in a 21st century context, might refer to as *people pleasing.*

[136] Original: *carry their cup.*

[137] 1 Peter 5:5.

[138] Ephesians 5:21.

[139] SPR Note: In the original, this phrase is, *And here meekness is of use either to injoyn silence, or to indite a soft answer.* Since I have changed the wording of these, the following titles (under "*First*" and "*Second*") will be changed as well.

First, to call for silence.[140]

It is declared that employees are to please their employers well in everything, not arguing[141] for that would be displeasing. It is better to say nothing than to say something that starts an argument. When our hearts are filled with anger, it is good for us to remain silent and hold our peace just as David did, and when he did speak, it was in prayer to God[142] and not in response to the wicked people before him.[143]

If the heart is angry, angry words will only add to the flame, just as wheels are heated by rapid motion.

One comeback or snarky response inspires another, and the beginning of a debate is like the release of water. It is difficult to stop the flow of water when the smallest crack is found in the dam.[144] Therefore, meekness says, "By all means, remain silent, and let the matter go! It is best to do this before it becomes an argument."

When a fire is started, it is good, if possible, to smother it and prevent it from spreading. We must be wise and stifle it immediately, or else the fire could get out of hand and be too great for us to put out.

Anger in the heart is like the books stored in the cellars of London homes during the great fire which, though they grew

---

[140] Original: *to injoyn silence.*

[141] Titus 2:9. SPR Note: the original uses the terms *servants* and *masters*, but from here on I will mostly aim to use the terms *employees* and *employers* or similar, more contemporary language.

[142] Psalm 39:2-3.

[143] *Quid refert inter provocantem & provocatum, nisi quod ille prior in maleficio deprehenditur, et ille posterior: nulla verò in maleficio ordinis ratio est.* Tertul. do Divin. c. 10. Transl. *For what difference is there between provoker and provoked, except that the former is detected as prior in evil-doing, but the latter as posterior? ... In evil doing there is no account taken of order...*"Tertullian, On Patience, Chapter X: On Revenge. https://catholiclibrary.org/library/view?docId =Synchronized-EN/anf.000081.Tertullian.OnPatience.html&chunk.id= 00000023. Accessed Apr. 5, 2025.

[144] SPR Note: The original used the phrase, *the least breach is made in the bank*, but *dam* feels more quickly understood by contemporary ears.

very hot at the time, did not burn until they were exposed to air many days later. As the heat was vented, the books burst into flame.[145] When the spirits of people are agitated, it may take a great deal of effort and pain to stifle the anger. However, even though the stubborn emotions resist the bridle, yet it will mean no remorse later on.

Those who find themselves wronged or hurt believe that they have the right to speak up about it, but it is better to be silent than to speak wrongly and to have to repent later. In those moments, the one who holds his tongue, holds his peace. And if we reflect on this kind of thing with a clear mind, we will find that we have often made things worse by speaking too much, but rarely do we make things worse by our silence.[146]

This must be remembered and followed, especially by those who serve others as they will certainly find the most comfort in meekness and patience and silent submission, not only when serving under good and gentle people, but also when serving under difficult[147] employers. It is good in such times to remember our place, and if the employer turns against us, we should not abandon our submissive position[148] or do

---

[145] *The Great Fire of London was a major conflagration that swept through the central parts of London from Sunday, 2 September to Thursday, 6 September 1666. The fire gutted the medieval City of London inside the old Roman city wall.* https://artsandculture.google.com/entity/great-fire-of-london/m0374t. Accessed April 5, 2025.

[146] *Complures vidi loquendo pecetum incidisse, vix quenquam tacendo: ideo{que} tacere nosse quàm loqui difficilius est.* Ambrde Offic. l. 1. c. 2. Trans. *How many have I seen to fall into sin by speaking, but scarcely one by keeping silent; and so it is more difficult to know how to keep silent than how to speak.* Ambrose, On the Duties of the Clergy, Chpt. 2, 5. https://www.newadvent.org/fathers/34011.htm. Accessed Apr. 5, 2025.

[147] Original: *froward*, meaning *contrary, unmanageable, difficult to deal with, having an evil disposition.*

[148] *Locus tuus patientia est, locus tuus sapientia est, locus tuus, ratio est, et sedatio indignationis.* Ambr. ubi supra. c. 21. Trans. *Your ground is patience, it is wisdom, it is reason, it is the allaying of indignation.* Ambrose, On the Duties of the Clergy, Chpt. 21, 92. https://www.newadvent.org/fathers/34011.htm. Accessed Apr. 5, 2025.

anything inappropriate, because "calmness will lay great offenses to rest."[149]

We have a proverb that teaches us this truth: "When thou art the hammer, knock thy fill; but when thou are the anvil, lie thou still."[150] It is the position God has placed you in that fits you best.

Even truth that is necessary to be said, if spoken in anger, may do more harm than good and offer more offense than satisfaction.

If others are angry with us without cause, even though we have the rational position, it is often best to delay justifying ourselves, though it feels necessary, until the emotion of the situation dies down. There is nothing said or done in emotionally charged situations that isn't better said or done after. When we are calm, we are likely to say it and do it better, and when our brother is calm, we will likely say it and do it with a better result.

Truth that is necessary to be said, if spoken in anger, may do more harm than good and offer more offense than satisfaction.

Even the prophet himself refrained from speaking a message from God when he saw King Amaziah in anger.[151] Sometimes it is wise to get someone else to speak the necessary words, rather than say them ourselves. However, we have a

---

[149] Ecclesiastes 10:4.

[150] SPR Note: This proverb has been left in its original wording.

[151] 2 Chronicles 25:16.

righteous God to whom, if in meek silence we allow ourselves to suffer injury, we can commit our cause, having his promise that he will "bring forth [our] righteousness as the light, and [our] justice as the noonday."[152] We are better off to leave it in his hands than try to handle it all ourselves. What we might call "clearing up the matter," God might call arguing with our brethren.

David was greatly upset by those who sought to hurt him and who spoke awful things against him, and yet he says, "I am like a deaf man; I do not hear, like a mute man who does not open his mouth."[153] And why did he hold his tongue? It was not because he had nothing to say or did not know how to say it, but because "for you, O Lord, do I wait; it is you, O Lord my God, who will answer."[154]

If God hears, I then have no need to hear. His involvement in the matter supersedes our own, and he is working towards justice, owning every righteous cause where there might be injury. However, he is also honourably engaged with showing up for those who, in obedience to the law of meekness, commit their cause to him. If there is any judgement or avenging necessary—and infinite wisdom is the best judge of that—God can do it better than we can. Therefore, "leave it to the wrath of God,"[155] that is, to the judgement of God, which according to truth and equity, allows God to take the seat of judgement. Because of this, we should never step in before him.

And it is proper that our wrath should defer to his, "for the anger of man does not produce the righteousness of God."[156] Even proper appeals to him, if they are made in moments of extreme emotion, are not welcomed into the court

---

152 Psalm 37:6.
153 Psalm 38:13.
154 Psalm 38:15.
155 Romans 12:19.
156 James 1:20.

of heaven as they are not brought forward properly. That one thing, that error, is enough to overrule them.

Those who do good and suffer for it should not spoil their own vindication by speaking or acting out of turn or by acting improperly.[157] Instead they should walk in the steps of the Lord Jesus who, when he was reviled, did not revile back; when he suffered, he did not threaten back, but was as a lamb, silent before the shearers, committing himself to the God who judges righteously.[158]

It is indeed a foundation part of self-denial to be silent when we have things to say and have the justification to say it.

It is indeed a foundational part of self-denial to be silent when we have things to say and have the justification to say it. If we control our tongues out of a pure regard for peace and love, it will not only turn out well, but it will also be evidence that we are truly Christ's disciples, having learned to deny ourselves.

It is better, by silence, to yield to our brother—one who is, has been, or may be our friend—than to yield to the devil through angry speech, as he is, has been, and ever will be our sworn enemy.

Second, to give a soft answer.[159]

---

[157] Original: *spoil their own vindication by mis-timing and mis-managing it.*

[158] Isaiah 53:7; 1 Peter 2:23.

[159] Original: *to indite a soft answer.*

Solomon encourages us that a soft answer is an effective way to turn away wrath, while harsh words stir up anger.[160] When someone speaks angry words to us, we must pause and think deeply on an answer, finding one that is mild and gentle enough for the situation before us and then present it in a mild and gentle manner.

When there is a fire, this kind of meek response pours water on the flames, while a stubborn argumentative response[161] pours oil onto the fire! Therefore, death and life are in the power of the tongue;[162] it is either for healing or killing, an antidote or a poison, all according to how it is used. When the waves of the sea beat against a rock, they batter the rock and make a terrible crashing noise, but soft sand receives the waves silently and returns them without damage.

A soft tongue is a wonderful gift[163] and carries a very unique virtue with it. Solomon declares that a soft tongue "will break a bone."[164] What this means is that a soft tongue will benefit those who are provoked and make them pliable. The one with the soft tongue will then "heap burning coals on [the] head"[165] of an enemy, not to *burn* him, but to *melt* him.

We say, "hard words break no bones,"[166] but it seems soft ones do, and yet they also do no harm as they calm an angry spirit and prevent it from growing angrier. A stone that falls on a pile of wool will remain there rather than bouncing away

---

[160] Proverbs 15:1.

[161] Original: *peevishness and provocation* which seems, in this context, to suggest a stubborn and emotionally inciting response.

[162] Proverbs 18:21.

[163] Original: *a wonderful specific* which in older English emphasizes the quality of the soft answer in regards to the tongue.

[164] Proverbs 25:15.

[165] Proverbs 25:21-22.

[166] SPR Note: This idiom is a shortened version of the more common, *Sticks and stones will break my bones...*, and it has been in use for centuries to essentially remind us that words actually have no power to do physical damage to us.

to do more damage; a meek answer accomplishes the same to an angry question.

It is observed in the battle between the Royal Tribe and the other ten that "the words of the men of Judah were fiercer than the words of the men of Israel."[167] When emotions rise, God (whose eyes are on all the ways of men) takes note of who speaks *fiercely* and sets a *mark* upon them.[168]

The good effect of a soft answer and the bad consequences of an argumentative one are observed in the stories of Gideon and Jephthah. Each of them, in the day of their triumphs over the enemies of Israel, found themselves in an argument with the Ephraimites.[169] This happened when the danger was past and the victory already won, because Ephraim had not been called upon to join in the battle. Gideon pacified them with a soft answer. "What have I done now in comparison with you?" In this, he magnified their achievements and downplayed his own. Speaking honourably of them and humbly of himself, he then says, "Is not the gleaning of the grapes of Ephraim better than the grape harvest of Abiezer?"[170]

In his reply, it is difficult to know if there is more wit or wisdom, but the effect it had on the situation was good. The Ephraimites were pleased, their anger turned away, a civil war prevented, and no one could think less of Gideon for his mildness and self-denial. In fact, the opposite happened in that he won more true honour by his victory over his emotions

---

[167] 2 Samuel 19:43. SPR Note: The original appears to reference 2 Samuel 14:43, a verse which, to my eternal chagrin, does not appear to exist in the Bibles available to me at this point in history. In other words, *someone done messed up.*

[168] SPR Note: Not all original versions include this paragraph.

[169] SPR Note: Some versions include, *an angry sort of people it seems* here as well as add a footnote, *Hence we read of the envy of Ephraim,* Isaiah 11:13.

[170] Judges 8:2.

than he did by his victory over all the hosts of Midian. The one who has control over his own spirit is better than the mighty.[171]

The Angel of the Lord pronounced Gideon a "mighty man of valour,"[172] and when he showed such tame submission before Ephraim, that did not at all detract from that part of his character.

Now Jephthah, on the other hand, who was known to be a man of rough and hasty spirit, even though he is in the list of the most esteemed believers[173]—for not all good people have the same temperament—responded differently than Gideon. When the Ephraimites argued with him just as they had with Gideon, Jephthah mocked them, criticized them for their cowardice, boasted of his own courage, and challenged them to justify their argument.[174]

They responded by insulting Jephthah's people, as is typical with strong emotions to taunt and mock, saying, "You are fugitives of Ephraim, you Gileadites."[175]

From words, this devolved into blows, and so great a flame did this little fire kindle that the only way to quench the fire was to spill the blood of forty-two thousand Ephraimites.[176] All of this could have been happily avoided if Jephthah had even half the meekness in his heart as he had reason on his side.

A soft answer is *the words* and *the way* of speaking this wisdom from above, the wisdom which is peaceable, gentle, and open to reason.[177]

To recommend this wisdom to us, we have the example of good men. One such example is found in Jacob's response

---

[171] Proverbs 16:32.
[172] Judges 6:12.
[173] Hebrews 11:32.
[174] Judges 12:2-3.
[175] Judges 12:4.
[176] Judges 12:6.
[177] James 3:17-18.

towards Esau. Though no one is more difficult to be won over than an offended brother, yet, just as Jacob prevailed with God by faith and prayer, so he prevailed with his brother by meekness and humility. We also have the pattern of angels who, even when a rebuke was needed, dared not pronounce a blasphemous judgement, but instead said, "The Lord rebuke you,"[178] as that passage is commonly understood.

And we have the example of a good God, who, although he could bring a charge against us with his great power, even so, he gives soft answers. Consider his interaction with Cain when that man was angry, and Cain's face fell. God reasoned with him, "Why are you angry? If you do well, will you not be accepted?"[179]

In the same way, he spoke with Jonah, "Do you do well to be angry?"[180] This is also shown in the parable of the prodigal son by the conduct of the father towards the older son who was so angry he would not come into the party. The father did not say, "Then let him stay out there!" but he went out himself and pleaded with him when he could just as easily have intervened with his authority. But, in meekness, he said, "You are always with me."[181]

When a highly emotional contest between two people has begun, a plague breaks out. The meek man, like Aaron, takes his censer with the incense of a soft answer, steps in quickly, and puts a stop to the plague.

Now, a soft answer in times when we are at fault—though hopefully we are not at fault to the degree that we are under criminal charges—must be repentant, humble, and submissive. We must be ready to acknowledge our error and not remain in sin or insist upon our own defence. Instead, we should

---

[178] Jude 1:9.
[179] Genesis 4:6-7.
[180] Jonah 4:4-9.
[181] Luke 15:28, 31.

exaggerate our sin, rather than excuse it, condemn ourselves rather than justify.

Humbling ourselves before our brothers and sisters, therefore, functions as good evidence of our repentance towards God. In the same way, if we are ready to forgive those who have offended us, that attitude of the heart functions as good evidence of our having been forgiven by God. Such surrender pacifies great offences.

Meekness teaches us to, as often as we trespass against our brother, to turn and say, "I repent."[182] An acknowledgement of our sin in the case of an intentional offense caused to others is perhaps as necessary to receiving a pardon as perhaps restitution is in the case of sin.

This is all, so far, the opening of our discussion on the nature of meekness, and we will now further illuminate this topic as we consider more specifically what is implied in *Quietness of Spirit.*

3. Quietness of Spirit

Quietness is the even nature, the composure, and the state of being in which the soul is at rest. Quietness speaks of both the nature and the excellency of the grace of meekness.

The greatest comfort and happiness of man is sometimes expressed by quietness. That peace in our conscience that Jesus Christ has left as a legacy for his disciples, that easily found sabbath of the soul which is a promise of the rest that remains for the people of God [183] is called "quietness and trust forever"[184] and is promised as the result of righteousness. "My people will abide in a peaceful habitation."[185]

---

182 Luke 17:4.

183 Hebrews 4:9-10.

184 Isaiah 32:17.

185 Isaiah 32:18. Some original versions do not include this reference to v. 18.

This is how gracious God is! He has happily pursued what is truly best for us by commanding us to do the very thing that he proposes and promises to us as a privilege!

We can justly declare that we serve a good Master whose "yoke is easy."[186] In fact, it is not only easy, but sweet and gracious, as the word "easy" indicates, and it is not only tolerable, but pleasing and acceptable. Wisdom's ways are not only pleasant, but they are pleasantness itself, and all her paths are peace.[187]

Quietness is the even nature, the composure, and the state of being in which the soul is at rest.

It is the character of the Lord's people, both in respect to holiness and happiness, that however they are branded as the troublers of Israel, they are the "quiet in the land."[188]

If every saint is a spiritual prince,[189] having a greater dignity than others and a deeper control over himself, surely he is like Seraiah, "a quiet prince."[190] This position is one of reigning with Christ, the transcendent Solomon, under the influence of the One who holds the golden scepter, through whom "peace abound[s], till the moon be no more."[191] And

---

[186] Matthew 11:30.

[187] Proverbs 3:17.

[188] Psalm 35:20.

[189] Revelation 1:6.

[190] Jeremiah 51:59. SPR Note: The KJV translates Seraiah's position as a *quiet prince* while the ESV translates his position as *quartermaster*.

[191] Psalm 72:7.

truthfully, even longer than that because "of the increase of his government and of peace there will be no end."[192]

Quietness is recommended as a grace with which we should be endowed, and a duty we should practise. Amidst all the abuse and injuries that are or can be put upon us, we must keep our spirits settled and undisturbed, and prove it by calm, even, and proper behaviour, showing that quietness is true in us.

This is quietness.

Our Saviour has declared that peacemakers will be blessed with adoption as sons,[193] and David professes himself to be that kind of a person, a peacemaker,[194] as opposed to those who delight in war.[195]

Now, if love is for the purpose of peace-making, surely this love begins at home[196] and is for making peace there, first and foremost. Peace in our own souls is in a large way conformity to the example set by the God of peace, who, though he doesn't always give peace on this earth, yet he always "makes peace in his high heaven."[197]

Some believe the primary intention of that peacemaking on which Christ declares a blessing[198] is to have a strong and robust affection for peace, to be peaceably minded.[199] This points to a bent and inclination of the soul. If one lies, he tends towards lying. If one makes peace, he is drawn to peace. This

---

[192] Isaiah 9:7.

[193] Matthew 5:9.

[194] Psalm 120:7.

[195] Psalm 68:30.

[196] SPR Note: The original states, *Charity begins at home* which was a common proverb. However, since the meaning of *charity* at the time of the original writing of this book was *love* it makes more sense to adjust this proverb to a contemporary reading.

[197] Job 25:2.

[198] Matthew 5:8.

[199] Dr. Hammond, A Practicall Catechisme. p. 125.

desire for peace is to have a disposition in the soul which is ready *to call for peace* whenever there might be a disturbance.[200]

To sum it all up, quietness of spirit is the soul's stillness and silence as it attempts to avoid provoking anyone or resenting provocation from anyone else.

Now, this summing up contains within it a bit of a metaphor, one which admirably illustrates the grace of meekness.

a. Quietness of the Air

First, we must be as quiet as the air on a calm day.

Disorderly emotions are like stormy winds in the soul, they toss it around and drive it quickly from place to place, often stranding it in lonely places or tipping it over. These emotions move the soul "as the trees of the forest shake before the wind," [201] which is the prophet's comparison, an apt illustration of a man in the extremes of emotion.

Meekness, however, restrains these winds and says to them, "Peace! Be still!"[202] and in this way maintains a calm in the soul and conforms it to him who has the winds in his hands and is therefore to be praised because even the stormy winds fulfil his word! A brisk wind is often useful, especially to the ship of desire, as the Hebrew phrase states in Job 9:26. So also in the soul there should be such warmth and vigor that will help speed us to the desired harbour.

Of course, it is not good to sit wind-bound[203] in a state of drowsiness or indifference. Tempests are dangerous, even when the wind blows in the right direction. So also are strong

---

[200] SPR Note: Not all original versions include the last four sentences in this paragraph.

[201] Isaiah 7:2.

[202] Mark 4:39.

[203] SPR Note: To be *wind-bound* is to be prevented from sailing in your desired direction by a strong, contrary high wind.

passions, even in good men. These extremes of emotions hinder the voyage and threaten the ship.

A life of quietness should be what we all work for, and meekness will contribute a great deal towards it. Meekness will silence the noise, control the force, calm the attack, and correct excessive and disorderly emotions.[204]

What manner of grace is this that even the winds and the sea obey it?[205] If we are willing to use the authority that God has given us over our own hearts, we can keep the winds of passion under the command of faith[206] and reason. When this is done, the soul is quiet, the sun shines, all is pleasant, tranquil, and smiling, and we sleep sweetly and safely, sheltered from the wind.

Keep in mind that we make our voyage among rocks and quicksand. If the weather is calm, we can more easily steer to avoid these hazards, and by care and control, avoid the extremes. However, the one who allows the winds of passion to gain control and spreads a large sail out before them will, while trying to avoid one rock, crash upon another. That man is in danger of being drowned in ruin and utter destruction by many senseless and harmful desires,[207] especially those that come from wars and battles.

b. Quietness of the Sea

Second, we must be quiet as the *sea is quiet from the waves.*

The wicked man's sin and punishment both lie in the unruliness of his own soul and the violence and disorder of his

---

[204] *Æolus sis, affectuum tuorum.* Neiremb. Trans. *Rule your passions, as Æolus rules the winds.* SPR Note: This quote appears to be a saying created by M. Henry and is quoted in his commentary on Proverbs 16:32. Æolus was the Greek god of the wind, so just as Æolus restrained the winds, we must restrain our angry passions.

[205] Matthew 8:27.

[206] SPR Note: The original uses the word *religion* here.

[207] 1 Timothy 6:9.

own emotion, and it might also not be the least of all his eternal torment. He is compared to "the tossing sea; for it cannot be quiet, and its waters toss up mire and dirt."[208] Men like this are not at ease with themselves nor with all around them, being "wild waves of the sea, casting up the foam of their own shame." And what is this foam of their own shame? It is the harsh things that ungodly sinners have spoken against God and the glorious ones, the things that they do not understand, and their loud-mouthed boasting and scoffing.[209]

Now, meekness is a grace of the Holy Spirit, the One who moves upon the face of the waters [210] and quiets them, smoothing out the rough sea and stilling the loud noise of its storms,[211] so that it no longer stirs up the mire and dirt of extreme emotions. The waves then no longer mount up to heaven[212] in proud and self-glorifying boasting; they do not go down to the depths to scrape up vile and abusive language. There is no reeling to and fro as drunk men or men in their rage.[213] There is none of that emotion that brings them to the end of their rope, but they are "glad that the waters [are] quiet, and he brought them to their desired haven."[214]

This calmness and evenness of spirit makes our passage over the sea of this world safe and pleasant, quick and speedy towards the desired harbour, pleasing and commendable in the eyes of others.

c. Quietness of the Land

Third, we must be quiet as when the *land is quiet from war.*

---

[208] Isaiah 57:20.

[209] Jude 1:8-18.

[210] Genesis 1:2.

[211] Psalm 65:7.

[212] Psalm 107:25-26.

[213] Proverbs 20:1. *If wine is a mocker and strong drink a brawler, anger is no less so.*

[214] Psalm 107:26-30.

In Asa's time, it was happily observed that "in his days the land had rest."[215] In the days of those who reigned before Asa, there was no peace for anyone who went out or came in, whether outward or homeward bound, they were exposed to terrible trouble.[216] But now, the rumours and alarms of war were stopped, and the people delivered from the noise of archers in the places of drawing water, as when the land had rest during Deborah's time.[217]

This is the kind of quietness that should be in the soul, a quietness where meekness rules the heart. A soul inflamed with wrath and passion at all times is like a kingdom at war, a civil war. They are subject to continual fighting, loss, and peril. Death and terror in its most horrible form walks victoriously. Sleep is lost, families broken, friends suspected, enemies feared, laws ignored, buying and selling ruined, business neglected, and cities wasted.

Ungoverned anger pours out this conflict and destruction, heap upon heap, when it is let loose in the soul. But meekness brings an end to these wars, breaks the bow, cuts the spear, and sheathes the sword. Amidst a contentious world, meekness preserves the soul from being the seat of war, and it makes peace within her lands. The quiet rest of the soul, then, is not disturbed, its comforts are not lost, its sense of control is not in disorder, and in this state, the laws of religion and reason rule, rather than the sword. With meekness in the soul, neither is union[218] with God nor with the saints disrupted, and temptation does not break in nor does corruption flow out of the soul. There is no complaining in the streets—no occasion given or taken to complain.

The soul that is in this state is happy.[219]

---

[215] 2 Chronicles 14:1-5.

[216] 2 Chronicles 15:5. SPR Note: from *whether outward...* to the end of the sentence is not included in all copies of the original.

[217] Judges 5:11 KJV.

[218] Original: *communion.*

[219] Psalm 144:14-15.

The words of a wise man "heard in quiet are better than the shouting of a ruler among fools. Wisdom is better than weapons of war."[220] This is the quiet everyone should work for, and it is what we can attain, if we would support and exercise the authority of the grace given to us to guide and control the power of the extreme emotions in our soul.

d. Quietness of a Child

Fourth, we must be quiet like a child is *quiet after weaning.*

The Psalmist lays out this comparison, "I have calmed[221] and quieted my soul, like a weaned child with its mother; like a weaned child is my soul within me."[222]

While a child is in the process of weaning, it is perhaps a little angry, difficult, and troublesome for a time, but once it is fully weaned, it quickly adjusts to the new way of feeding. In the same way, when a quiet soul is provoked by the denial or loss of some earthly comfort or delight, it quiets itself and does not worry, nor does it trouble itself with anxious cares about how to live without that comfort. Instead, it decides to make the best of the situation.[223]

Now, this holy indifference to the delights of the self is, similar to the experience of a weaned child, a good step towards becoming a "perfect man, unto the measure of the stature of the fulness of Christ."[224] A child recently weaned is

---

[220] Ecclesiastes 9:17-18.

[221] *or rather "I have composed," so Ainsworth reads it...*

[222] Psalm 131:2.

[223] SPR Note: Some original versions include the following statements at this point: *If wormwood be put upon the breasts, which we have call'd the breasts of our consolation, it is but to make us indifferent to them, and we must set our selves to answer that intention, and sit loose to them accordingly.*

[224] Ephesians 4:13. Additional Note from some versions: *Yet corrupt Passions appear betimes. Vidi zelantem parvulum qui intuebatur pallidus amaro aspectu collactaneum suum.* Aug. Conf. 1, 7. Extended translation (of more of the text): *I myself have seen and known an infant to be jealous though it could not speak. It became pale, and cast bitter looks on its foster-brother.* Augustine,

free from all the unease and unrest of care, fear, anger, and revenge. Its sleep is undisturbed, and even while dreaming, the child appears pleasant and smiling. Its days are easy; its nights are quiet.

If the child falls into a bad mood now and then, it fades away quickly, the upset forgiven, the entire experience soon forgotten, and all of it buried under an innocent, loving kiss. Thus, if ever we would enter the kingdom of heaven, we must be converted from pride, envy, ambition, and a striving to be ahead of others. Instead, we must become like little children.[225] This is what our Saviour told us, Who, even after his resurrection, is called "the holy child Jesus."[226]

And even when we have put away other childish things, when it comes to malice, we must still be children![227] And regarding the arguments of other people, a meek and quiet Christian seeks to have no interest in such things and to be as unengaged in them as a weaned child might be in his mother's arms, incapable of holding such angry resentment.

This is the meekness and quietness of spirit which is recommended to us:

> We are to have such a command and composure of our soul that it is unable to become unhinged by any provocation whatsoever. Instead, all its powers and faculties

---

Confessions. https://www.newadvent.org/fathers/110101.htm. Accessed April 10, 2025.

[225] *Et si citò pueri inter se moventur, facilesed antur & majri suavitate in se recurrunt; nesciunt se subdole artificioseque tractare.* Amb. de Of fic. l. 1. c. 21. Translation: *And if boys quickly come to quarrel one with the other, they are easily calmed down again, and quickly come together with even greater friendliness. They do not know how to act deceitfully and artfully.* Ambrose, On the Duties of the Clergy. https://www.newadvent.org/fathers/34011.htm. Accessed Apr. 10, 2025.

[226] Acts 4:27 KJV.

[227] 1 Corinthians 14:20.

are to remain under control in anticipation of
the time when it is proper to respond.[228]

Simply stated, put away all wrath, anger, and malice, those corrupt appendages of the old man. Dig up and throw away all those roots of bitterness, and stand guard constantly against all the improper extremes of your own emotion.

If you do this, then you will quickly know, to your own comfort, better than I can tell you, what it is to be of a meek and quiet spirit.

---

[228] Colossians 3:8.

II

The Excellency
of Meekness

Now, one might think the first chapter of this book should be enough to carry the entire topic, and the explaining of the nature of meekness and quietness should be enough to help us to understand how profitable it is.[1]

We can see such a wonderful sweetness in this topic in our very first reading about it that if we look upon the beauty of meekness, we cannot help but be enamoured with it! But because our corrupt hearts oppose both this and all graces of the Holy Spirit, I will endeavour more carefully to show how excellent this grace is, so that we can come to the point, if possible, of falling in love with it and submitting our souls to the charming power of meekness!

---

[1] SPR Note: This is perhaps especially true considering Chapter One takes up approximately one quarter of the entire book!

It is said that a man of understanding has an excellent spirit.[2] Tremellius translates that phrase as "he is of a *cool* spirit,"[3] and if we put them together, we learn that a cool spirit is an excellent spirit. A man of understanding is governed by this kind of spirit!

Scripture tells us—do we need more than God's Word?—that it is *of great price in the sight of God*, and we can be sure that anything precious in the sight of God, truly is precious! What God declares as good *is* good, very good, because his judgement is according to truth. Sooner or later he will bring all the world in line with his own mind, and our end will be whatever he has decided it will be. And he will be "justified in [his] words and blameless in [his] judgement."[4]

So for us, we will be able to understand how excellent a meek and quiet spirit is if we consider four things: the *honour* of it; the *comfort* of it; the *benefit* of it; and how it *prepares us for future blessings*.

1. The Honour of a Meek and Quiet Spirit

Consider how honourable a meek and quiet spirit is. Everyone desires honour and reputation, though very few properly consider what these qualities are or the appropriate way to obtain them. To add to this, few people believe there is much true honour in the grace of meekness. They also do not consider how successful the path is that mild and quiet souls take to gain the approval of their Master and of their fellow-

---

[2] Proverbs 17:27 KJV.

[3] Immanuel Tremellius, Testamenti Veteris Biblia Sacra, p. 163, 1603. *frigidus spiritu* or *cold spirit*. https://archive.org/details/testamentiveteri00trem/page/n515/mode/2up. Accessed Aug. 30, 2025.

[4] Psalm 51:4.

servants who love God, those who are like their Father in heaven.

Now, let us see what honour there is in meekness.[5]

a. The Honour of a Victory

What a great story [6] the names of high and mighty conquerors tell in the records of fame! Their conduct, their valour, and their successes are proclaimed and celebrated! But, if we are willing to believe the word of truth and pass judgement according to its standard, "whoever is slow to anger is better than the mighty, and he who rules his spirit than he who takes a city."[7]

Behold, someone who is greater than Alexander or Caesar is here. The former, some believe, lost more true honour by yielding to his uncontrolled anger than he gained by all his conquests. There is no victorious chariot so comfortable, so safe, so truly glorious as the chariot in which meek and quiet souls ride across all the provocations of an abusive world. They ride in this convoy with a gracious lack of concern or stress as there is no convoy so splendid or so noble as that convoy of comfort and grace that rides with this chariot!

The conquest of an uncontrolled passion in our hearts is more honourable than the conquest of an uncontrolled people in a nation. The reason for this is the battle over passions require more true courage. It is easier to kill an enemy outside yourself, which can be defeated with a blow, than to chain up and rule an enemy within, which requires a constant, even, steady hand, and a long and consistent effort to bring it under control.

---

[5] SPR Note: Not all original versions include this sentence.

[6] Original: *figure*. SPR Note: I have adjusted this phrase from the original and added a metaphor (story/tell) as it fits and communicates the original concept in a more contemporary manner.

[7] Proverbs 16:32.

A good example of this kind of thing is found with David. He received more honour by yielding and by allowing himself to be conquered by Abigail's words than by conquering Nabal and all his house.[8] For a rational, reasonable person, a rational victory will always be considered more honourable than a brutal victory, and this rational victory ends up being an affordable, safe, and unbloody conquest that does no harm. No lives and no treasures are sacrificed to it. The glory of these triumphs are not stained, as others generally are, with funerals.

It is easier to kill an enemy outside yourself, which can be defeated with a blow, than to chain up and rule an enemy within.

Every battle of the warrior, says the prophet, is "in battle tumult and every garment rolled in blood."[9] The meek man's victory, however, will be achieved by the Spirit of the Lord of hosts. In meek and quiet suffering, we are "more than conquerors through [Christ] who loved us."[10]

We are conquerors who have lost little. In fact, we lose nothing but the gratifying of a base lust. Instead, we are conquerors who gain so much! The spoils of war that we divide are very rich: the favour of God, the comforts of the Spirit, the foretastes of everlasting pleasures. These are more glorious and excellent than the mountains of prey.[11] We are more than conquerors! We are actually celebrators! We live a life of

---

[8] 1 Samuel 25.
[9] Isaiah 9:5.
[10] Romans 8:37.
[11] Psalm 76:4.

victory; every day is a day of triumph to the meek and quiet soul.

Meekness is a victory over ourselves and over the rebellious lusts in our own hearts. It is the quieting of the internal battles and the stilling of personal rebellions, which is often harder than to resist a foreign invasion. It is an effective victory over those who do us wrong and set themselves as our enemies, and it is often a means to win their hearts.

The law of meekness is:

> If thine enemy hunger, feed him;
> if he thirst, *propina illi.*

Propina illi[12] means to "tip to him." So, if your enemy is hungry, feed him, if he is thirsty, not only give him a drink—which is an act of charity—but drink to him as an act of friendship, true love, and reconciliation. In doing this, you will "heap burning coals on his head."[13] Not to consume him, of course, but to melt and soften him, that he may be cast into a new mould. And so, while the angry and revengeful man, who will take down everyone before him with a heavy hand, is overcome with evil, the patient and forgiving man will overcome evil with good.[14] For "when a man's ways please the Lord, he makes even his enemies to be at peace with him."[15]

Meekness is even a victory over Satan, the greatest enemy of all. What conquest can be more honourable than that? In Scripture, we read a beautiful verse, one that has been written as a caution for us. This verse reflects honour on those who conquer through grace: "For we do not wrestle against flesh and blood, but against the rulers, against the authorities,

---

[12] *Propina* is the Spanish word for "tip" and *illi* is the Latin word for "to him".

[13] Romans 12:20.

[14] Romans 12:20-21.

[15] Proverbs 16:7.

against the cosmic powers over this present darkness."[16] As we magnify the adversary, we magnify the victory over him.

These are the meek man's vanquished enemies. The spoils of these battles are the trophies of victory.[17] It is truly the intentions of the devil—that great deceiver and destroyer of souls—that are disgraced. It is his attack that is defeated, and his assault that is pushed back by our meekness and quietness.

Our Lord Jesus was more admired for controlling and commanding the unclean spirits than for any of the other healings. Unruly passions are unclean spirits, legions of which possess some souls, and in the lives of their victims, these unruly passions bring about a hopelessness and lead towards ungodly extremes. The soul then becomes like that man who cried out and cut himself with stones,[18] or the boy who was so often cast into the fire and water.[19]

The meek and quiet soul is, through grace, a conqueror over these enemies—their fiery darks are quenched by the shield of faith.[20] Satan is then, in some measure, trodden under foot, and the victory will soon be complete when "the one who overcomes"[21] will sit down with Christ upon his throne, even as Christ overcame and sat down with the Father on his throne. In this place of honour, he still appears in the image of his meekness, "a Lamb... as though it had been slain."[22] And upon Mount Zion, at the head of his heavenly hosts, he also appears as a Lamb.[23]

---

[16] Ephesians 6:12.

[17] Ἕνα μόνον ἐχθρὸν ἔχε τὸν Διάβολον, πρὸς αὐτὸν μηδέποτε καταλλάττα, πρὸς ἀδελφὸν μηδέποτε ἀπεχθῶς ἔχε. John Chrysostom, Homily 20 on the Statutes. https://www.newadvent.org/fathers/190120.htm. Accessed Sept. 6, 2025.

[18] Mark 5:3-5.

[19] Mark 9:22.

[20] Ephesians 6:10-20.

[21] Revelation 21:7.

[22] Revelation 5:6.

[23] Revelation 14:1.

Such is the honour that meekness has in those higher regions.

b. The Honour of Beauty

The beauty of a thing consists in the symmetry, harmony, agreeableness of all the parts. And what is meekness? Is it not the soul's agreement with itself?

Meekness is the joint cooperation of all the affections working towards the universal peace and quiet of the soul, every affection working in its own place and order and therefore contributing to the common good. Next to the beauty of holiness, which is best understood as agreement with God, is the beauty of meekness. And this beauty of meekness is the soul's agreement with itself.

This beauty of meekness is the soul's agreement with itself.

"Behold how good and pleasant it is" for the powers of the soul to "dwell in unity."[24] In this state, the reason knows how to rule and, at the same time, the affections know how to obey. Deviant emotions are strife in the soul. It is like a tumour on the face, spoiling the beauty. Meekness drains the fluids, brings down the swelling, prevents the deformity, and preserves the beauty.

This is one instance of the attractiveness of grace, "through my [beauty]," says God to Israel, "which I had put upon thee." [25] This grace of meekness puts a charming

---

[24] Psalm 133:1.
[25] Ezekiel 16:14 KJV.

loveliness and an admirable quality upon the soul which renders it acceptable to all who know what true worth and beauty is. The one who in righteousness, peace, and joy in the Holy Spirit—that is, in Christian meekness and quietness of spirit—"serves Christ is acceptable to God and approved by men."[26]

And who else is there anywhere to whom we wish to be accepted?

Solomon, a very competent judge of beauty, determined that "a man's wisdom makes his face shine,"[27] and doubtless the meekness of wisdom contributes as much as any aspect of wisdom to this splendor.

We read of three people in Scripture whose faces shone brightly, and they were all examples of meekness. The face of Moses shone,[28] and he was the meekest man on the earth.[29] The face of Stephen shone,[30] and he is someone who, while under a shower of stones, so meekly submitted and prayed for his persecutors.[31] The face of our Lord Jesus shone[32] in his transfiguration, and he was a perfect pattern of meekness.

This grace of meekness causes a sweet and pleasant breeze to pass over our countenance, while it keeps the soul in tune and frees it from those jarring disagreements which come because of ungoverned emotions.

c. The Honour of an Adornment

The Apostle speaks of the honour of meekness as an adornment much more excellent and valuable than gold,

---

[26] Romans 14:17-18.
[27] Ecclesiastes 8:1.
[28] Exodus 34:30.
[29] Numbers 12:3.
[30] Acts 6:15.
[31] Acts 7:60.
[32] Matthew 17:2.

pearls, or costly attire. It is an adorning of the soul, an adoring of the source, the immortal part of a man. Outward adornments do nothing but cover and beautify the body. Of course, the body is really not much more than a sister to the worms and will one day be a feast for them. But we speak of being adorned with this beautiful ornament[33] of the soul, and by this we are connected to the spiritual world.[34] This is an adorning that hands us over to the care of God, an adorning which, in his sight, is "of great price."[35] This is wonderful as we know that the value of an ornament is based on the appraisal, and there is nothing greater than God's appraisal.[36]

God is the one who sets the standard! Those who are righteous [37] are righteous before God, and a beautiful ornament is beautiful if he declares it to be. It is a beautiful ornament of God's own making. Is the soul dressed up in beauty? If so, God is the one who has dressed it this way!

By his Spirit, God has painted the heavens with beauty, and by this same Spirit, he has painted the meek and quiet soul. The soul is a beautiful ornament, acceptable to him. And… of course it is, since he has accomplished this work in us! For everyone who has the beautiful ornament of God's work in their lives, more beauty will be added to it.

He has promised that he will adorn "the humble with salvation," [38] and if the clothes of salvation will not make someone beautiful, what will? The robes of glory will be the everlasting beautiful adornments of meek and quiet spirits.

---

[33] Archaic meaning: An *ornament* in this context is not simply an object, but something that adds to the beauty of something else. While I have kept this word at times, in many instances I changed this word to *adornment*.

[34] Original: *invisible world.*

[35] 1 Peter 3:4.

[36] Original: *Ornaments go by estimation.* SPR Note: The original phrase did not offer much to go on, but in context, this reading appears to fit the intention.

[37] Luke 1:6.

[38] Psalm 149:4.

This meekness is an adornment that, like the Israelites' clothing in the wilderness, will never wear out, nor will it ever go out of fashion as long as rational thought and good religion have their place in the world. All the wise and good people will see those who have put on the Lord Jesus Christ as the ones who are the best dressed, and those who walk with Jesus will be seen as wearing the pure clothing [39] of meekness and innocence. Even Solomon in all his glory was not dressed like these lilies of the valley,[40] though we are lilies among thorns.

Now, this same beautiful ornament of meekness recommended to wives in 1 Peter is also recommended to all of us by the same apostle, calling us to be subject to one another.[41] This command points out what meekness is! It is the mutual yielding which we owe to one another for edification, and it is motivated by our fear of God.[42]

This feels like a difficult saying. How are we to take this in? An infeasible task! How are we to conquer it?

Well, the answer is in the text. "Clothe yourselves, all of you, with humility."[43] This calling to humility implies *first* the unchangeableness of his grace. We must belt it tightly around our waist and not let it hang loose, or else it might be snatched away by every temptation. If we wish to remain watchful and resolute in the strength of Christ, we must tie the knot on this belt of grace, making it a tight belt that holds secure. *Second*, the beauty and the wonderful ornament of this humility is to be put on as a knot of ribbons, a decoration, as an ornament to the soul. This is the meekness of wisdom. It gives us an

---

[39] Original: *white.*

[40] Matthew 6:29.

[41] 1 Peter 5:5 KJV.

[42] Ephesians 5:21.

[43] 1 Peter 5:5. Note from original: την ταπεινοφροσυνην εγκομβωσασθε, innodate, from κομβος, a knot: *The word is, innodate, from a knot.* Additional Note: *Vobis infixam abete. Erasm.* Transl. *Fix within you.*

ornament of grace to wear on our heads and, even more, a crown of glory![44]

d. The Honour of True Courage

Meekness is typically despised by the high and mighty of our day.[45] They tend to view it as cowardice. It is considered undignified, morally flawed, and evidence of immaturity,[46] and when they talk about it, this is the way they present it. At the same time, they celebrate and applaud furious and angry revenge under the wonderful names of valour, honour, and greatness of spirit. This comes from a poor understanding of courage, the true nature of which is stated ingeniously:

> It is a resolution never to decline any evil of pain when the choosing of it, and the exposing of ourselves to it, is the only remedy against a greater evil.[47]

Therefore, if someone is threatened and runs forward into sin—which is the greater evil—out of fear of shame and reproach, he is the coward. However, someone who is

---

[44] Proverbs 1:9; 4:9.

[45] Original: *grandees* referring to high ranking nobles, powerful people, people of social influence. Additional Note: *Magni animi est proprium, placidumesse & injurias superne despicere.* Sen. Tranlsation: *Now it is the property of a great mind to be calm and tranquil and to look down upon outrages and insults with contempt.* Lucius Annaeus Seneca, Seneca the Younger, On Clemency, Book I, Chpt. 5. to Nero Caesar. https://standardebooks.org/ebooks/seneca/dialogues/aubrey-stewart/text/on-clemency. Accessed April 14, 2025.

[46] Original: *little soul* which appears to refer to a child. I have taken this to point to immaturity.

[47] Norris, Miscell. (John Norris) A Collection of Miscellanies, Of Courage, p. 168. https://quod.lib.umich.edu/e/eebo/A52417.0001.001?rgn=main;view=fulltext. Accessed June 16, 2025.

threatened and allows himself to be shamed out of fear of sin,[48] he is a man of courage!

True courage is the mental conviction that enables a man to suffer rather than to sin,[49] to choose affliction rather than iniquity,[50] to walk away from an attack, even if he loses as a result and is called a fool and a coward, rather than engage in a sinful argument. If a man can deny the brutal lust of anger and revenge rather than violate the royal law of love and kindness, regardless of how opposite it is from the world's approach, he is resolute and courageous. "The Lord is with you, O mighty man of valour."[51]

Worry and stress is the fruit of the weakness of women and children, while it falls short of the strength of a man, especially of the new man who is born from above. When our Lord Jesus is described in his majesty, riding victoriously, the glory he has is "truth and meekness and righteousness."[52]

The courage of those who overcome this great red dragon of wrath and revenge by meek and patient suffering and by loving "not their lives unto the death,"[53] will find a good and honourable welcome on the other side of the grave. There they will be crowned with glory and honour and immortality[54] while those who spread their terror in the land of the living will fall miserably, "and they bear their shame with those who go down to the pit."[55]

---

[48] *Paul showed more true valor when he said, I can do nothing against the truth, than Goliath did when he defied all the host of Israel.* Ward (Poss. Seth Ward—1617-1689—but it is difficult to know for sure who "Ward" might be).

[49] Hebrews 11:25-26.

[50] Job 36:21.

[51] Judges 6:12.

[52] Psalm 45:4.

[53] Revelation 12:11.

[54] Romans 2:7.

[55] Ezekiel 32:24.

e. The Honour of a Conformity to the Best Patterns

The image of those who are admittedly excellent and glorious contains an excellence and glory within it. To be meek is to be like the greatest of the saints, the elders who obtained a good reputation and were of renown in their generation. To be meek is to be like the angels whose meek interaction with and service to the saints is easily seen in the Scriptures.

No, wait! Meekness is more than that!

To be meek is to be like the great God himself whose goodness is his glory.[56] He is "slow to anger"[57] and he has "no wrath."[58]

Therefore, we are followers of God, dear children, when we "walk in love" [59] and are "kind to one another, tenderhearted, forgiving one another."[60] The more quiet and sedate we are, the more like God we are. Even though he is intimately involved in all the affairs of this world, he is far from being moved by its convulsions and revolutions.[61] As he was from eternity, so he is and will be to eternity, infinitely content in his own joy of himself.

The Scripture speaks to his praise and glory, "The Lord sits enthroned over the flood[s],"[62] even when the floods have

---

[56] *Who* is *Deus Optimus* (transl: *God is the best*), and therefore *Maximus* (God the Great).

[57] Exodus 34:6; Numbers 14:18.

[58] Isaiah 27:4.

[59] Ephesians 5:2.

[60] Ephesians 4:32.

[61] *The Hebrew criticks observe, that in the name, all the letters are quiescent.* SPR Note: This footnote is a reference to the letters of God's name (YHWH) which were not pronounced out of reference/fear for the name of God. Therefore, as *silent* letters, they symbolize here that in a world of chaos, God is at rest/peace, and we should be like him.

[62] Psalm 29:10.

lifted up their voices and lifted up their waves.[63] This is the
eternal mindset, that he sits as firm and undisturbed on a
rushing flood[64] as he sits on an immovable rock. He is the
same yesterday, today, and forever. The meek and quiet soul,
therefore, that preserves its peace and calm against all the
upsetting insults of passion and provocation ends up in some
way participating in that divine nature![65]

Now, let the true honour that comes with this grace of
meekness entrust this meekness to us. This meekness is
something that is honourable, pure, lovely, commendable, and
worthy of praise—a praise not necessarily of men, but of
God.[66] This is a guaranteed way to receive and keep perhaps
not a great name, but indeed a good name. This is the kind of
name that is better than precious ointment.[67]

Keep in mind, there will be those who walk all over the
meek of the earth and look on them as Michal looked on
David, despising them in their hearts.[68] Yet even so, if this is
considered vile by the people of the world, let us be even more
vile and inferior—as much as we can!—and we will find, as
David argues, that there are those who hold us in honour.[69]

---

[63] Psalm 93:3-4.

[64] *Quad disideras magnum & summum est, Deoque vicinum, non concuti.* Sen. Transl. *But what you desire is something great and supreme and very near to being a god—to be unshaken.* Seneca the Younger. On the Tranquility of the Mind. https://trisagionseraph.tripod.com/Texts/Tranquility.html. Accessed Sept 4, 2025.

[65] 2 Peter 1:4. Additional Note: *Diis proximus ille est. Quem ratio non ira movet.* Claudius. *What you want is, that noble, that divine attainment—unshaken tranquillity.* SPR Note: This may be a reference to a concept from Shakespeare's Hamlet referring to Claudius's refusal to act on the murder of Polonius.

[66] Philippians 4:8; Romans 2:29.

[67] Ecclesiastes 7:1.

[68] 2 Samuel 6:16.

[69] 2 Samuel 6:22.

For the word of Christ will not fall empty to the ground. Whoever "humbles himself will be exalted."[70]

**The best way to find rest
for our souls is to learn
from Jesus who is gentle
and lowly in heart.**

2. The Comfort of a Meek and Quiet Spirit

Consider, for a moment, how comfortable a meek and quiet spirit is.

What is true comfort and pleasure but a quietness in your own heart? Those who are at peace within themselves are peaceful to others, while those who are a burden and terror to all those around them will certainly be the same way in their own hearts. If someone wishes to lead a quiet life, they must lead a peaceful life,[71] and the best way to find rest for our souls is to learn from Jesus who is "gentle and lowly in heart."[72]

Let our "reasonableness be known to everyone… and the peace of God which surpasses all understanding will guard your hearts and your minds."[73] Quietness is the thing that even the busiest and noisiest people of the world pretend to desire and pursue. They claim they will be quiet and expect it to be

---

[70] Matthew 23:12.
[71] 1 Timothy 2:2.
[72] Matthew 11:29.
[73] Philippians 4:5, 7.

so, or they set out to find out why it isn't quiet.[74] Because of this, they will not endure from others even the smallest disturbance of their quietness.

To add to the absurdity of it all, they run madly around in circles in their effort to pursue quietness, but in the process, they greatly disturb their own personal, inward quietness, putting their souls into a continuous uproar. And they do all this simply to prevent or fix some small noise from someone else.

But the meek man finds a sweeter, safer *quiet*, and he finds there a greater comfort than what those who vainly pursue *quiet* find. "Great peace have those" who love this law of love, for "nothing can make them stumble."[75] Whatever offense is intended by those who cause upset, the meek do not receive it or interpret it that way, and by this, peace is preserved. If there is a heaven anywhere on earth, it exists within the meek and quiet soul that moves and breathes above that difficult realm infested with storms and violent winds. The harmony of a meek soul is like the famous "music of the spheres"[76]—a perpetual melody.

"Steadfast love and faithfulness meet; righteousness and peace kiss each other."[77]

To understand this further, we examine how a meek and quiet Christian will live very comfortably for he enjoys *himself*, he enjoys his *friends*, he enjoys his *God*, and he lives in a way that even *his enemies are unable to disturb him* in his enjoyment.

---

[74] SPR Note: This section in the original was particularly difficult to decipher in terms of the context. *They will be quiet—this is their claim—yea, that they will, or they will know why.*

[75] Psalm 119:165.

[76] SPR Note: The concept of the Music of the Spheres is a philosophical (and perhaps spiritual) concept originating with Pythagoras (approx. 570 to 495 BC). It posits the idea that there is a musical harmony in the celestial bodies.

[77] Psalm 85:10.

a. He Enjoys Himself

Meekness is close friends with the endurance our Lord Jesus commanded us as necessary to the saving of our own souls.[78] How calm are the thoughts, how peaceful are the affections, how rational the future hope, and how even and composed are all the decisions of the meek and quiet soul.[79] A meek man is free from the pain and torture of an angry man who is robbed of himself—a man who he works and strives to gather possessions as he loses his own soul.

The angry man's reason is like a mist. It cannot argue, infer, or foresee with any certainty. His affections are at full speed, driven by an engine that is as uneasy as it is dangerous.

Who is the righteous man who is comfortable with himself?[80] Who else but the quiet man who does not need to travel around to find satisfaction, but having Christ dwelling in his heart by faith has inside him the peace which the world cannot give or take away.

While those who are filled with worry and anger rise early in the morning and stay up late at night, eating the bread of anxious toil as they pursue revenge, the God of peace gives sleep to "his beloved."[81]

The sleep of the meek is quiet, sweet, and undisturbed. Those who by innocence and by mildness are the sheep of Christ will be made to "lie down in green pastures."[82] Those

---

[78] Luke 21:19.

[79] *Opinion is the rate of things, From whence our peace doth flow, I have a better fate than kings, Because I think it so.* Katherine Phillips, A Country Life, https://quod.lib.umich.edu/e/eebo2/A54716.0001.001/1:8?rgn=div1;view=fulltext. Accessed June 5, 2025.

[80] Proverbs 14:14. Additional Note: *Ne te quaesiveris extra.* Transl. *Do not seek outside yourself.* SPR Note: This phrase is often attributed to the poet Heraclitus (roughly 540-480 BC) and emphasizes looking inward for answers.

[81] Psalm 127:2. Additional Note: *Jedidiah, one of Solomon's names, who was a man of peace.* 2 Samuel 12:25.

[82] Psalm 23:2.

things that might break an angry man's heart will never break the sleep of a meek man.

It is promised that the meek "shall eat and be satisfied."[83] He finds a certain sweetness in the common comforts, while the angry man is never satisfied. Either he cannot eat, his stomach is too full, his stomach is too arrogant,[84] or he eats and is not satisfied.[85]

It is referred to as the happiness of the meek that they "delight themselves in abundant peace."[86] There are those who delight themselves in great wealth, a poor delight indeed, and it comes with so much trouble and restlessness, but the meek, though they have very little money, have peace, a great amount of peace, peace like a river,[87] as much as they have the heart to enjoy!

"They have light within,"[88] as Œcolampadius said, "their souls are a Goshen in the midst of the Egypt of this world. They have a light in their dwelling when clouds and darkness are round about them."[89] This is the joy in which no stranger shares.[90] Truthfully, we will find less inner turmoil and more true ease and satisfaction through forgiving twenty offenses than avenging one, and we would do well to think about this truth! No doubt Abigail intended more than she expressed when, in her attempt to persuade David to ignore the insult from Nabal, she wisely suggested that "this shall have no cause

---

[83] Psalm 22:26 KJV.

[84] *as Ahab*, 1 Kings 21:4. Original: *too high.*

[85] *unless he can be revenged, as Hamam: "All this avails me nothing," though it was a banquet of wine with the king and queen, "as long as Mordecai is unhanged."* Esther 5:12-13 KJV.

[86] Psalm 37:11.

[87] Isaiah 48:18; 66:12.

[88] *at lucis intus.* SPR Note: Rough trans.: *but [there is] light within.*

[89] SPR Note: I was unable to find a definite reference to this quote, although a portion of this quote is found at the following link: https://www.studylight.org/commentaries/eng/jtc/hosea-4.html. Accessed April 16, 2025.

[90] Proverbs 14:10.

of grief or pangs of conscience."[91] Not only that, but with forgiveness, the memory is much more comfortable.

In fact, this is all such a good thing, especially in difficult times, to have the testimony of a clear conscience. We can walk in innocence and godly sincerity, not with worldly wisdom, but by the grace of God—particularly the grace of meekness. By God's grace, we can walk in this world so as to please God and do our duty, because God does not agree with the words of the unbelievers, "Revenge is sweeter than life,"[92] for it often proves more bitter than death.[93]

b. He Enjoys His Friends

Enjoying our friends is one of the most wonderful joys of life. We were intended to be social creatures, and a Christian should be even more so. An angry man, however, is unfit to be social as he bursts into flame at every upset. He is better suited to be abandoned to the lions' dens and the mountains of the leopards[94] than to walk in the footsteps of lambs.[95]

If someone has their hand raised against every other man, he not only holds Ishmael's character, but also Ishmael's fate, "everyone's hand against him,"[96] and therefore lives in a state of war. But meekness is the cement of society, the bond of Christian unity. It smooths out and polishes the bricks and fits them tight together. These bricks are living stones which are

---

[91] 1 Samuel 25:31.

[92] *Est vindicta bonum, vitâ jucundius ipsâ.* Transl. *O! but vengeance is good, sweeter than life itself.* Juvenal, Satire XIII. Translation by G. G. Ramsey. https://www.tertullian.org/fathers/juvenal_satires_13.htm. Accessed Sept. 5, 2025.

[93] SPR Note: This final sentence was particularly difficult to rephrase into contemporary English. Here is the original: *He did not speak the Sense, no not of the sober Heathen, that said, Est vindicta bonum, vitâ jucundius ipsâ: Revenge is sweeter than Life, for it often proves more bitter than death.*

[94] Song of Solomon 4:8.

[95] Song of Solomon 1:8.

[96] Genesis 16:12.

built into a spiritual house to be like the stones of the temple that Herod built, all as one stone. While "Hard upon hard," as the Spanish proverb goes, "will never make a wall."[97]

Meekness preserves a unity that is like the precious oil on the holy head and the dew on the holy hill.[98] In our current state of imperfection, we can maintain no friendship, agreement, or proper social interaction without mutual compromises with one another. We do not yet dwell with angels or the spirits of faithful men and women made perfect, but with others who struggle with evil passions just like us. Meekness teaches us to keep this in mind and to respond to people accordingly, and with this in mind, distances, divisions, feuds, and quarrels are all easily prevented and even the beginnings of these arguments are quickly and intentionally crushed.

It is necessary to true friendship to surrender our extreme emotions, and to subject these emotions to the rules of friendship. Perhaps this is what is revealed through the story of Jonathan when he gave to David his sword, bow, and belt—all his military equipment—as he entered a covenant with him.[99]

c. He Enjoys His God

Enjoying God is certainly the most satisfying part of meekness! It is the perfect form of all happiness, and without this enjoyment, all our other enjoyments are tasteless and uninteresting.

---

[97] SPR Note: I was unable to find an early source for this old Spanish proverb, however, its meaning is that stubbornness and conflict are not constructive to progress.

[98] Psalm 133:1-2.

[99] 1 Samuel 18:1-4.

No one is more qualified to truly enjoy God than those who are clothed with "the imperishable beauty of a gentle and quiet spirit, which in God's sight is very precious."[100]

When the Psalmist had conquered an unruly passion and pulled himself together, he lifted up his soul to God in a righteous and humble cry, "Whom have I in heaven but you? And there is nothing on earth that I desire besides you."[101] We enjoy God when we see and believe the evidence of his favour and hold on to the assurance that it is ours. When we experience in our hearts the reception of his grace and the continual experience of his image stamped upon us, we are not only left able to taste his love, but we also own a token of that love. Those who are the most meek and quiet usually have this benefit more than others.

There are none more qualified to truly enjoy God than those who are clothed with "the imperishable beauty of a gentle and quiet spirit."

In our anger and extreme emotions, we give room in our lives to the devil and incite God to pull back from us. Nothing grieves the Holy Spirit of God, the One through whom we have fellowship with the Father, more than "bitterness and wrath and anger and clamor and slander."[102] But this is the one

---

[100] 1 Peter 3:4.
[101] Psalm 73:25.
[102] Ephesians 4:31-32.

to whom God will look: "he who is humble[103] and contrite in spirit and trembles at my word."[104]

The great God sets aside heaven and earth to focus with favour on the meek and quiet soul. In fact, he not only *focuses on them*, but he *dwells with them*.[105] This points out the constant interaction and relationship between God and humble souls. His secret is with them. He gives them more grace, and those who dwell in love, dwell in God and God in them.

The waters were dark, but they were quiet when the Spirit of God moved over them, and out of them, God produced a beautiful world.[106]

This calm and peaceful posture qualifies and prepares us for receiving and entertaining a visit from the divine, and it sets boundaries around the mountain on which God is to descend,[107] so that there might be no interruption while Moses speaks with God. It also calls the daughters of Jerusalem "by the gazelles and does of the field," those sweet, gentle, and peaceful creatures, to "not stir up or awaken love until it pleases."[108]

Some believe that when Elisha called for the "musician" that it was for the calming and composing of his spirit, since he appeared to be a little ruffled or upset. After which, the "hand of the Lord came upon him."[109]

Never was God more intimate with any mere man than he was with Moses, the meekest of all the men on the earth.[110] This meekness was a necessary qualification of the high priest

---

[103] *To him that is quiet, so the Syriac—to him that is meek, so the Chaldee.* SPR Note: *Syriac* and *Chaldee* are references to different translations/texts of the Old Testament and how they translate/record this verse.

[104] Isaiah 66:2.

[105] Isaiah 57:15.

[106] Genesis 1 (specifically v. 2).

[107] Exodus 19:12.

[108] Song of Solomon 2:7.

[109] 2 Kings 3:15.

[110] Numbers 12:3.

who was to draw near to minister as it would enable him to have compassion on the ignorant and on those who have strayed from God.[111]

The Lord will guide the meek in judgement[112] with a still, small voice [113] which cannot be heard when the extreme emotions are loud and stormy.

The angry man, when he awakes, arises with the devil, contriving some malicious scheme. The meek and quiet man, however, when he awakes, arises with God, comforting himself in the reality of God's favour.

"Return, O my soul, to your rest,"[114] said David when he considered himself to be among the humble, that is mild, innocent, and inoffensive people. Return to your Noah, for Noah's name means *rest*. Perhaps this meaning alludes to the *rest* the dove found with Noah in the ark when she could find nowhere else to land. [115] Those who are as harmless and humble as doves can return to God as comfortably as they can return to rest.

This is excellently paraphrased by Mr. Patrick:[116]

God and thyself (my soul) enjoy in quiet rest,
freed from thy fears.

It is said that "the Lord lifts up the humble."[117] As long as their meekness remains in control, they are lifted above the storms and secured in a perpetually calm and peaceful sphere. Those who are at home with God and live a life of communion with him, not only in the serious ordinances of the faith but

---

[111] Hebrews 5:1-2.

[112] Psalm 25:9.

[113] 1 Kings 19:12.

[114] Psalm 116:7.

[115] Genesis 8:8-9.

[116] *Mr. Patrick* likely refers to Bishop Simon Patrick (1626-1707). Bishop Patrick was a Bible commentator.

[117] Psalm 147:6.

even in the regular difficulties and experiences of the world, are certainly exalted! Every day is a Sabbath, a holy rest for the meek and quiet soul. It is as a day spent in heaven! As the grace of meekness takes root in our lives, the comforts of the Holy Spirit grow stronger and stronger, just as God has promised in his word: "The meek shall obtain fresh joy in the Lord, and the poor among men shall rejoice in the Holy One of Israel."[118]

d. He Is Unable to be Disturbed

The enemies of a meek man are powerless to disturb and interrupt him in these enjoyments. His peace is not only sweet but safe and secure. As long as he acts within the law of meekness, he is beyond the reach of attacks from those who wish to cause trouble. He who dwells quietly under "the shelter of the Most High" will surely be delivered "from the snare of the fowler."[119]

The greatest attacks men can make would not hurt us[120] if we did not, by our uncontrolled and foolish concern, come within reach of their canon.[121] If we welcome these attacks, we have no one to blame but ourselves when we are hurt.[122] The one who has learned to forgive hurts and let them go with meekness and quietness has found the best and surest way of thwarting and defeating those hurts.[123] In fact, it's actually a form of innocent revenge.

---

[118] Isaiah 29:19.

[119] Psalm 91:1, 3.

[120] *Nemo laeditur nisi à seipso.* Dict. Diogen. Transl. *No one is harmed except by themselves/No man is hurt but by himself.* SPR Note: This saying is attributed to Diogenes the Cynic (approx. 412-323 BC).

[121] SPR Note: ...*and within reach of their canon* is not in all original texts, despite the fact that the sentence makes far less sense without it.

[122] Original: *we may therefore thank ourselves if we be damaged.*

[123] *Idcirco quis te laedit ut doleas, quia fructus laedentis in dolore laesi est, ergo, cum fructumejus everteris non dolendo, ipse doleat necesse est amissione fructûs sui Improbum caedis sustinendo.* Tertull. de patientiâ cap. 8. Transl. *No doubt the reason why anyone hurts you is that you may be pained; because the hurter's enjoyment*

There was evidence, then, that King Saul was moved by a different spirit when the children of Belial despised him and brought him no gifts, hoping to rattle his newly formed government by their contempt. However, "he held his peace" and as a result, neither his soul nor his crown was disturbed.[124] When Shimei cursed King David, he intended to pour vinegar into his wounds and to add affliction to the afflicted, but David, by his meekness, held his peace, and Shimei's plans were foiled. So, "let him curse!"[125] Poor Shimei hurt himself more than David who, while he kept his heart from being tinder for those sparks, was no more affected by the verbal attacks than the moon is by the foolish dog that barks at it.

The meek man's prayer is like that of David, "Lead me to the rock that is higher than I,"[126] and there I can, as Mr. Norris expresses it:

—smile to see
The shafts of fortune all drop short of me.[127]

The meek man is like a ship at anchor—he is *moved* but not *removed*. The storm will move a meek man's ship—the meek man is not simply a wooden post or a stone—but he cannot be *removed*. In the same way that faith quenches

---

consists in the pain of the hurt. When, then, you have upset his enjoyment by not being pained, he must needs he [sic] pained by the loss of his enjoyment. Then you not only go unhurt away, which even alone is enough for you; but gratified, into the bargain, by your adversary's disappointment, and revenged by his pain. Tertullian, On Patience, Chapter 8. https://www.newadvent.org/fathers/0325.htm. Accessed April 19, 2025. SPR Note: This translation is not a direct translation as the Latin ends with something along the lines of, ...be pained by the loss of his enjoyment by enduring the death of the scoundrel. I could not find that last phrase, so I included a portion of the rest of the paragraph instead.

[124] 1 Samuel 10:27.
[125] 2 Samuel 16:10-11.
[126] Psalm 61:2.
[127] John Norris, A Collection of Miscellanies, The Retirement, Part V. https://quod.lib.umich.edu/e/eebo/A52417.0001.001?rgn=main;view=fulltext. Accessed June 16, 2025.

temptations in general, meekness is a grace that (in reference to the pressures of attacks and hurts) quenches the fiery darts of the wicked.[128] Meekness is an armor that is tested to stand against the spiteful and poisoned arrows of attack and is an unbreakable wall that secures the peace of the soul, a place where no thief can break through to steal. While this is how a meek man lives, in contrast the angry man lays all his comforts at the mercy of every wasp that will try to sting him.

So therefore, overall, it appears as though the ornament of a meek and quiet spirit is as comfortable as it is beautiful.

3. The Immediate Benefit of a Meek and Quiet Spirit

Consider how beneficial a meek and quiet spirit is.

All people are focused on getting what they want. This is what a fast-paced world is fixated upon, "each to his own gain, one and all."[129] It is for this goal that people lose sleep and exhaust themselves.

Unfortunately, it will be difficult to convince that kind of person that there really is more to be gained through meekness and quietness of spirit than by all their upset and confusion. They firmly believe that "in all toil there is profit," yet God tells them, "In returning and rest you shall be saved; in quietness and in trust shall be your strength." They will not, however, take his word for it, but they say, "No! We will flee upon horses. We will ride upon swift steeds."[130]

---

[128] *Meekness is the greatest affront to all injuries in the world, for it returns them upon the injurious, and makes them useless, ineffective and innocent.* Jeremy Taylor, The Great Exemplar of Sanctity and Holy Life According to the Christian Institution. https://archive.org/details/greatexemplar02tayl/page/n3/mode/2up?q=meekness. Accessed June 5, 2025.

[129] Isaiah 56:11. SPR Note: Not all original versions include this entire sentence.

[130] Isaiah 30:15-16.

The One who came from heaven to bless us has guaranteed a special blessing on the grace of meekness. "Blessed are the meek,"[131] and when he says they are blessed, that makes them blessed! For everyone whom God blesses is blessed indeed. Not only are they blessed *already*, but they *will* be blessed!

Meekness is therefore profitable and beneficial.

a. The Condition of the Promise

There is, however, a condition to this promise of receiving the wonderful benefit. Christ promises that the meek "shall inherit the earth," and this is quoted from Psalm 37:11. In the entire New Testament, this is almost the only express promise of a temporal benefit.[132] Now, this is not to say that they shall receive only the earth, for that would mean they are not truly blessed. Instead, they have a promise of something more.

Some read this promise as they will inherit the land of Canaan. However, the land of Canaan was not only a type and figure, but to those who believed, it was a token and pledge of the heavenly inheritance. So then,

> The blessings from God for the meek man are so great that even two Canaans (earthly and heavenly) are barely large enough to contain them all. The same intense happiness that Adam would have had in paradise belong to the meek, so they will have a life here of paradise followed by an easy move to heaven for eternity.[133]

---

[131] Matthew 5:5.

[132] *As heaven is taken by violence, so is earth by meekness. Trap. in loc.*

[133] Henry Hammond, A Practicall Catechisme. p. (mihi) 117. https://quod.lib.umich.edu/e/eebo/A45443.0001.001?rgn=main;view=fulltext. Accessed Apr. 24, 2025. Original: *A double Canaan is thought little enough for the meek man; the same felicity in a manner attending him which we believe of Adam, if he had not fallen—a life in paradise, and thence a transplantation to heaven.*

A Discourse on Meekness

Meekness is a branch of godliness which offers, more than any other branch, a "promise for the present life."[134] They shall inherit the earth!

The sweetest and surest ownership is that which comes through inheritance, that which holds its foundation in the position of sonship. Those things that come through being the heir are attributed by the law as an act of God, a gift from him, the very One who has a special hand in providing for the meek. They are his children, and if the meek are his children, then they are his heirs.

It is not as if the meek will be rich, as if their share will be the largest portion of the world's goods, but whether he has more or less, he has it by the best title! It's not by random, but by a covenant right. He holds *in Capite*,[135] in Christ our head, an honourable ownership.

If the meek man only has a little, he not only has it from God, but he also has it with God's blessing, therefore everything he has is pure, and he is at peace with it. As the wise man declared, "Better is a dry morsel with quiet than a house full of feasting with strife. Better is a dinner of herbs where love is than a fattened ox and hatred with it."[136] Even if food is scarce, the man who has control over his own spirit knows

---

SPR Note: This is a somewhat tricky section to rewrite in modern English. Another approach might be to say, *The blessings from God for the meek man cannot be contained in an earthly Canaan, but require a heavenly Canaan to fulfill all that is promised. The same intense happiness that...*

[134] 1 Peter 4:8.

[135] *Terram inhabitant quam sibi divinitus concessam esse norunt, & securè agunt sub Dei tutelâ, et hoc illis satis est donec mundi haereditatem ultio die adeant. Feroces vero omnia possidendo nihil possident.* Calv. in Mat. 5. 5. Transl: *They inhabit the earth which they know to be theirs by the divine allotment, and they are safe beneath the divine protection; this suffices them till, in the last day, they arrive at the full possession of their inheritance. The furious, on the contrary, by grasping at all, lose every thing.* Calvin, Matthew 5:5. https://www.ccel.org/c/calvin/comment3/comm_vol31/htm/ix.xli.htm. Accessed Apr. 24, 2025.

[136] Proverbs 17:1; 15:17.

how to make the best of it and to suck "honey out of the rock, and oil out of the flinty rock."[137]

"Blessed are the meek; for they shall wield the earth," so the old Wycliffe's Bible significantly translates it—as I remember it quoted in the Book of Martyrs. [138] Good management contributes more to our comfort than great possessions. Whatever a meek man has on this earth, he knows how to wield it, how to manage it, and how to make good and proper use of it! And he does this in every circumstance.

A quiet soul will inherit enough of the world that they are guaranteed to have as much of it as is good for them, as much as will help them to carry their responsibilities through in a proper and beneficial manner.[139] Who could ask for more?

The promise of God without owning the world is better than owning the world with no claim on the promise.

The promise of God without owning the world is better than owning the world but having no claim on the promise.

---

[137] Deuteronomy 32:13.

[138] Foxe's Book of Martyrs, 1563 AD.

[139] Original: *as much as will serve to bear their charges through this world to a better.* SPR Note: It is possible this is better understood as referring to children, in which case, a proper rephrasing might be, *as much as will help them raise their children in a way that is good for them.*

b. The Reception of the Promise

In its very nature, meekness offers a benefit and advantage in the here and now. "If you are wise, you are wise for yourself"[140] in this world, and you will effectively address your own interests.

i. Meekness Has a Good Influence on Our Health.

If "envy makes the bones rot,"[141] meekness preserves them. As the indulging of improper appetites (towards those things that satisfy the cravings of the flesh) corrupts a man, so also does the indulging of extreme emotions (against those things that upset) corrupt a man. These things harm and injure the very body that they fight so much to protect.[142]

The excesses and abnormalities of anger stir up those negative moods in the body and that kindles and increases degenerating and terminal diseases. Meekness, however, rules those moods and therefore contributes greatly to good emotions and proper functioning of the body.

When Ahab grew sick in his envy of Naboth's vineyard, meekness would have quickly cured him. [143] Moses, the meekest man, not only lived quite long, but was free from the infirmities of age. "His eye was undimmed, and his vigor unabated."[144] This strength and endurance may very well be attributed to his meekness.

The days of old age would not be such evil days if the elderly did not, by their own stubbornness and restlessness, make them worse than need be. Uncontrolled anger inflames the natural heat and so gives birth to diseases which come on

---

[140] Proverbs 9:12.
[141] Proverbs 14:30.
[142] SPR Note: Not all original versions include the last two sentences.
[143] 1 Kings 21.
[144] Numbers 12:3; Deuteronomy 34:7.

quickly. It dries up the radical moisture[145] and quickly brings on chronic sickness.

The body is called the sheath or scabbard of the soul.[146] How often does an envious, worry-filled soul cut through its own sheath (body) like a sharp knife, and like they say of the viper's brood, they eat their way out.

Meekness, however, prevents all this.

The quietness of the spirit will help to hold down depression, and this, along with other precepts of wisdom, will add health to the body and deep strength to the bones. "Length of days and years of life and peace they will add to you,"[147] but "vexation kills the fool."[148]

ii. Meekness Has a Good Influence on Our Wealth.

Meekness has a good influence on our wealth in terms of the preservation and increase of it. War brings poverty. It does this in kingdoms and even in families and neighbourhoods. Many have taken a wealthy estate and brought it to ruin by giving way to uncontrolled anger, that rude idol, to which even the children's food and the family's care is often sacrificed.

Contention will just as quickly clothe a man with rags as does laziness. Meekness, the very thing that keeps peace, is a close friend of wealth.

It was Abraham's meekness in his management of the quarrel with Lot that secured both his and Lot's possessions,

---

[145] SPR Note: *Radical moisture* is a Galenic physiological concept that posits there is a *radical moisture* in all living beings that is vital for life and present in the body from birth. By the time of Matthew Henry's birth, the concept was already largely rejected.

[146] Daniel 7:15. SPR Note: The word translated *body* in the KJV and *within me* in the ESV properly means *sheath* or *scabbard*.

[147] Proverbs 3:2.

[148] Job 5:2.

which otherwise would have been easy prey for the Canaanite and Perizzite who dwelt in the land.[149] And Isaac, whom I have sometimes thought to be the most quiet of the patriarchs, someone who lived most of the days of his pilgrimage quietly, raised the greatest wealth of any of them. He "gained more and more until he became very wealthy." [150] Even Jacob lost nothing in the end by his meek and quiet conduct towards his uncle Laban.[151]

Love is better than law; for love is cheap, but law is costly.

Revenge is costly. Haman paid dearly for it, no less than ten thousand talents of silver.[152] It is better to forgive and save the charges. Mr. Dod used to say, "Love is better than law; for love is cheap, but law is costly."[153]

When it comes to tradesmen, it is often seen that those who make the least amount of noise thrive the most. They are those who "do their work quietly" and mind their own business.[154]

---

[149] Genesis 13:7-8.

[150] Genesis 26:13.

[151] Genesis 29-31.

[152] Esther 3:9.

[153] Original: *law is chargeable.* SPR Note: This appears to be a paraphrase of John Dod's words: *it was better to buy love than law; for one might have a great deal of love for a little, whereas one could have but a little law for a great deal.* The Gleanings of Heavenly Wisdom: The Sayings of John Dod, p. 26, 1851.

[154] 2 Thessalonians 3:12.

iii. Meekness Has a Good Influence on Our Safety

In the day of the Lord's anger, the meek of the earth are most likely to be safe. It may be that you will be hidden, as in the promise.[155] In fact, if anyone is, you certainly will be. The meek man stands most likely to receive God's special protection!

Meekness is close to that kind of innocence that is often an effective protection against wrongs and hurts. Now, while some low and worthless people will be thrilled to harm the gentle and humble, it is obvious to all honourable people that attacking an unarmed, unresisting man, a man who does not fight back, is an act of cowardice. "Now who is there to harm you if you are zealous for what is good?"[156]

Who draws his sword or cocks his gun at the harmless, silent lamb? But everyone is ready to do it at the furious, barking dog.

This is how the meek man escapes many of those perplexing troubles, those distresses, sorrows, and unearned wounds, the very things that the angry, provoking, and revengeful man brings upon himself. Wise men turn away wrath, but "a fool's lips walk into a fight, and his mouth invites a beating."[157] It is an honour "for a man to keep aloof from strife, but every fool will be quarreling."[158]

I remember Mr. Baxter speaks of this in his book, Obedient Patience:

> Once going along London streets, a hectoring, rude fellow jostled him; he went on his way, and took no notice of it; but the same man affronting the next he met in like manner, he

---

[155] Zephaniah 2:3.
[156] 1 Peter 3:13.
[157] Proverbs 15:1; 18:6.
[158] Proverbs 20:3.

drew his sword and demanded satisfaction, and mischief was done.[159]

If a man would like to sleep in safety and with a clear conscience, he must learn to forgive hurts rather than revenge them. The two goats that met on the narrow bridge in Luther's fable were both in danger if they were to fight, but both were saved by the humility of the one that laid down and let the other go over him.[160]

The evil inherent in anger turns our friends into enemies, but it is the excellency of meekness that turns our enemies into friends, which is an effective way of conquering them.

Saul, an enemy as unrelenting as could be, was more than once melted by David's mildness and meekness. "Is this your voice, my son David?"[161] asked Saul. "I have sinned. Return, my son David."[162] And after that, Saul no longer persecuted him.[163]

The change that Jacob's meekness brought about in Esau is also easily observed, and some believe the change is seen in a strange and surprising manner by an unusual reference in the Hebrew text to Esau kissing Jacob.[164] It is revealed by a prick over every Hebrew letter to encourage the reader to pay special attention to it.

---

[159] Richard Baxter, Obedient Patience, https://quod.lib.umich.edu/e/eebo2/A76190.0001.001?rgn=main;view=fulltext. Accessed June 5, 2025.

[160] SPR Note: this fable is actually attributed to Aesop, not to Martin Luther, however, Luther refers to it in speaking about humility and avoiding conflict. This reference to the fable by Luther appears to be why M. Henry attributes it to Luther. Luther, Table Talk, of Discord, DCCXXXII, https://www.ccel.org/ccel/luther/tabletalk.v.xxxi.html. Accessed Apr. 24, 2025.

[161] 1 Samuel 24:16.

[162] 1 Samuel 26:21.

[163] 1 Samuel 27:4.

[164] Genesis 33:4.

Due to God's involvement in this world, some believe[165] it is quite true that during times of public trouble and calamity, the meek and quiet have fared the best out of anyone. Their portion of the trouble has been safe and easy, especially when compared with the fate of the riotous or rebellious.

Whoever is wise and considers these things will understand the lovingkindness of the Lord towards the quiet in the land, against whom we read of plots laid out and deceitful plans devised.[166] These plots and plans, however, are of no concern because by God's overruling providence, the plans are baffled, and they fail.

In this way, the grace of meekness carries with it its own reward. As we keep this commandment and even after it is kept, "there is great reward."[167]

4. The Ability for Meekness to Prepare us

Consider how meekness prepares us for something beyond today. It is very desirable for the faithful to "stand mature and fully assured in all the will of God,"[168] to be complete and "equipped for every good work,"[169] to be made "ready for the Lord a people prepared."[170]

An active movement of grace in your life is the best preparation for living out the entire will of God. Grace is what establishes the heart, it is the root of the matter, and a good foundation for what is to come. This grace of meekness is a

---

[165] Dr. *Hammond, A Practicall Catechisme. p.* 117. https://quod.lib. umich.edu/e/eebo/A45443.0001.001?rgn=main;view=fulltext. Accessed June 5, 2025.

[166] Psalm 35:20; 37:12, 14.

[167] Psalm 19:11.

[168] Colossians 4:12.

[169] 2 Timothy 3:17.

[170] Luke 1:17.

particularly good way to prepare ourselves for what lies before us in this world.

a. Meekness Makes Us Fit for Any Duty

The grace of meekness puts the soul in a state of readiness and keeps it there for aspects of the Christian faith. Just as there was no noise of axes or hammers in the building of the temple, those who are most fit for service in the temple are those people who are quiet and composed. The work of God is best done when it is done without noise.

Meekness qualifies and makes us ready to hear and receive the word of God. When malice and envy are set aside, and we are like newborn infants in terms of innocence and inoffensiveness, it is then when we are most fit to receive the sincere milk of the Word of God—and of course, most likely to grow as a result.[171] Meekness prepares the soil of the heart for the seed of the word, just as the farmer plows and breaks up the clods of dirt in the field and prepares the field. He can then sow the "wheat in rows and barley in its proper place."[172]

Christ's ministers are fishers of men,[173] but we seldom fish successfully in troubled waters. The voice that Eliphaz heard was ushered in with a profound silence while he lay in his bed at night, a quiet place and posture before the Lord.[174] God "opens the hearts of men, and terrifies them with warnings."[175]

Another duty which meekness disposes us for and enables us to perform properly and acceptably is prayer. We cannot lift up pure hands in prayer unless they are hands "without

---

[171] 1 Peter 2:1-2.
[172] Isaiah 28:24-25.
[173] Matthew 4:19.
[174] Job 4:16.
[175] Job 33:15-16.

anger."[176] Prayers made in wrath are written in bile and can never please or persuade a God of love and peace.

Our rule is to "first be reconciled to your brother, and then come and offer your gift."[177] And if we do not take this method, we will find that even though we seek God in due ordinance, we do not seek him in due order.[178]

The Lord's day is a day of rest, and no one is fit for it unless they are in a quiet state, one where our souls have entered into that real sabbath provided to the people of God through the gospel.[179] The Lord's supper is the gospel feast of unleavened bread which must be kept, not with the old leaven of wrath, malice, and wickedness, but with the unleavened bread of sincerity and truth.[180]

After the conflict between Abraham and Lot was over and Abraham had learned so much mildness and humility through the experience, God made a visit to Abraham.[181] The more

---

[176] 1 Timothy 2:8.

[177] Matthew 5:23-24. Additional Note: *Leave thy Gift* : Θεος υκ ήλειται ατιμιαν ειναι τοδωρο καταλιμτανομενα, και συνομίζεις ὑβριν, εἶναι, το προτερος απελθειν και καταλο --. *God does not deem that any dishonour attaches to him, when he leaves a gift, though it should be slighted; and dost thou think it degrading to make the first overture toward reconciliation!* Chrysostom, Homily 16 on Matthew. https://www.newadvent.org/fathers/200116.htm. Accessed Apr. 29, 2025.

[178] SPR Note: I left this sentence largely in the original language due to the word-play involved here. Perhaps a more modern reading might be, "...we will find that even though we can approach God freely according to his word, we will have done this out of order having not first reconciled to our brother."

[179] Hebrews 4:9.

[180] *Quid est ad pacem Dei accedere sine pace? ad remissionem debitorum cum retentione? quomodo placabit patrem iratus in fratrem, cùm, omnis ir- ab i-itio interdicta sic nobis?* Tertul. de Orat. c. 10. Transl: *For what sort of deed is it to approach the peace of God without peace? the remission of debts while you retain them? How will he appease his Father who is angry with his brother, when from the beginning "all anger" is forbidden us?* Tertullian, On Prayer, Chapter 11. https://www.documentacatholicaomnia.eu/03d/0160-0220,_Tertullianus, _De_Oratione_[Schaff],_EN.pdf. Accessed Apr. 29, 2025.

[181] Genesis 13:14. SPR Note: This sentence in the original reads: *God made a gracious visit to Abraham, and after that the strife between him and Lot was*

carefully we preserve the unity of the saints, the richer we are for unity with God.

The sacrifices God called for under the law were not ravenous beasts and birds of prey, but calves, young goats, lambs, turtledoves, and young pigeons, all pictures of meekness, gentleness, and inoffensiveness. These are sacrifices with which God is well pleased. This quietness of spirit contributes very much to the calmness and understandability of a religious life.

This quietness of spirit contributes very much to the calmness and understandability of a religious life.

Hot tempered and on-edge people who are ready to take aim at everything are usually very fickle in their profession of faith and are terribly inconsistent in their lives. They are like a very sick man, sometimes burning up, sometimes shivering with cold, or they are like those who gallop in the beginning of their journey and tire before the end of it. The meek and quiet Christian, however, remains constant, holding to a steady rate of speed and therefore making progress.

---

over, in which he had discovered so much mildness and humility. I believe the above rewrite is a proper rendering of the meaning, but an alternative reading could be, *After the conflict between Abraham and Lot had ended, God made a gracious visit to Abraham through which Abraham learned so much mildness and humility.* The difference between those two readings have to do with whether Abraham learned the mildness and humility through his experience with Lot or through his experience in the visit from God. Based on the context of the following sentences, I believe the rendering in the rewrite above to be accurate.

If the arm of the compass swings wildly around the circumference, you must be sure to keep the other arm fixed in place and steady in the centre, for your strength as a meek and mild person is to sit still.[182]

b. Meekness Makes Us Fit for Any Relationship

Meekness makes us fit for any relationship which God, in his leading, may call us to. Those who are quiet in their souls find they are at ease around everyone else, and the closer they are to us in relationship and activity, the more we will desire to be at ease in return. There are many types of relationships, those where we are in authority over others, those where we are under others, and those where we are of equal standing. Someone who is of a meek and quiet spirit gets along with all of them!

Moses was forty years a nobleman in Egypt, forty years a servant in Midian, and forty years a king in Jeshurun,[183] and not only did his meekness qualify him for each of these positions, but his meekness enabled him to hold fast to his integrity.

There are various duties required, depending on the relationship, and various graces to be lived out, but meekness is the golden thread that must run through all of them. If people are social creatures, the more kindness they exhibit, the better they fit in with society. Meekness greatly helps to preserve the wisdom and proper authority of those in authority, the obedience and proper submission of those under authority, and the love and mutual kindness of equals.

---

[182] Original for this sentence: *If you would have one foot of the compass go even round the circumference, you must be sure to keep the other fixed and quiet in the centre, for your strength is to sit still.*

[183] SPR Note: *A poetic name for the people of Israel. Deuteronomy 32:15.*

A Discourse on Meekness

A calm and quiet spirit gratefully welcomes the support of the relationship, pays close attention to the expectations, and bears the responsibilities and effort involved in the relationship—for everything comes with ups and downs—cheerfully and calmly.

I have heard of a married couple, both of whom were naturally quick to anger. Despite this struggle, they found a way to live together comfortably by holding to an agreement made between them: to never both be angry at the same time. This is an excellent law of meekness, which, if obeyed faithfully, would prevent many of the rifts among friends and relatives which brings on so much guilt and grief and rarely heals without scarring.

A devoted and ingenious father gave the following advice to his newly married children:

> Doth one speak fire? t'other with water come;
> Is one provoked ? be t'oher soft or dumb.[184]

Therefore, as one moves forward in wisdom, both can be happy. But where wrath and anger are indulged, all relationships are poisoned. Those relationships which should be there for support become like thorns in our eyes and sharp sticks in our sides. Two are certainly better than one,[185] yet even so it is better to live in a desert land than with a quarrelsome and fretful person[186] who is like "a continual dripping on a rainy day."[187]

---

[184] SPR Note: This quote is left in its original form as it carries a certain poetic flow and feel to it that I fear I cannot replicate in contemporary English. To prove this point, here is my rewrite, *Is one speaking fire? The other should blast them in the face with the fire hose. Is one angry? The other should just shut their face.* (I confess. Poetry is not my thing.)

[185] Ecclesiastes 2:9.

[186] Proverbs 21:19.

[187] Proverbs 27:15.

Some Hebrew critics have observed that if you take away the fear of the Lord from husband and wife, there only remains fire.[188] This is also the case in other relationships.[189]

c. Meekness Makes Us Fit for Any Situation

Meekness prepares us to handle any situation that the wise God might lead us into. Those who, through grace, are able to compose and quiet their hearts are fit to live in this world where every day we face so much that can rile us up and upset us. Generally speaking, whether situations arise that are good or bad and whether the world smiles or frowns on us, a meek and quiet person is neither raised up by one nor cast down by the other. Regardless of what happens, they maintain the same control. When our finances crumble and collapse or when our property increases, the mind does not rise or fall with it. In adversity, the meek man is encouraged, and when he is cast down, he does not despair.

St. Paul learned how "to be content" in whatever situation. He knew how to be brought low and how to abound. In every circumstance, he learned the secret of facing plenty

---

[188] Original: *Some of the Hebrew critics have noted, that if you take away* יה *the fear of the Lord, from* איש *and* אשה; *husband and wife there remains but* אש *and* אש *fire, fire.-It is so in other relations.* SPR Note: Not all texts contain this sentence, and I can see why. I will try to explain as best I can from my research (as Hebrew was never my strong point). The Hebrew word for the fear of the Lord is written with the letters *he geresh* יה (note: Hebrew reads from right to left so the order is actually *geresh he*, but for ease for English readers I will follow a left to right reading). In the Hebrew words for husband and wife, husband is spelled *shin-geresh-aleph* איש, while wife is spelled *he-shin-aleph* אשה. If the *he* and *geresh* יה (the fear of the Lord) is removed from the words for *husband* and *wife* איש and אשה (*he* ה from *wife* and *geresh* י from *husband*), we are left with two letters for each, *shin* and *aleph* אש which is the Hebrew word for *fire*.

[189] SPR Note: Not all original versions include this paragraph.

A Discourse on Meekness

and facing hunger, abundance and need. [190] The changes around him and in his experience made no change on the inside.

This is an emotional state in which, as far as it maintains command of the soul, makes every burden light by bringing the mind forward to consider the situation rather than let the situation overwhelm the mind.

Prosperity and adversity both have their own particular temptations towards stubborn and contrary natures. [191] Prosperity tends to lead people to try to control others, while adversity tends to lead people to be impatient of others.

Against the assault of each of these temptations, the grace of meekness will stand guard! To pass through this world "through honor and dishonor, through slander and praise," that is, through different kinds of conditions and as we are treated in different ways, we have need of that patience, kindness, and genuine love[192] which will be "the weapons of righteousness for the right hand and for the left."[193]

Meekness and quietness with fortify the soul on the right and left hand and prepare it for all that the world might throw at it. Meekness, then is like the careful ship's captain who, based on the point of the compass, will shift his sails to accommodate the wind, knowing both when to move forward and endure the storm and when to put down anchor and wait it out so as to not suffer damage.

With an ongoing contentedness, a heart at rest will make the best of whatever circumstance might come.[194]

---

[190] Philippians 4:11-12.

[191] Original: *peevishness and forwardness*. Perhaps another rewording might be *stubborn and disobedient.*

[192] Alternate reading: *...we have need of that genuine patience, kindness, and love...*

[193] 2 Corinthians 6:6-8.

[194] Μη ζητει τα γινομενα γινεσθαι ὡς θελεις, αλλα θελε γινεσθαι τα νινυμενα ὡς γίνεται, και εν ποιησεις. *Seek not to adjust events to your will, so much as to adjust your will to events; thus you will act a becoming part.* Epictetus, The

d. Meekness Makes Us Fit for a Day of Persecution

If tribulation and affliction arise because of the word of God—which is certainly not unusual—the meek and quiet spirit is already fully equipped with the proper armour. This armour preserves the spirit's peace and purity at such a time, which are our two primary concerns. This allows us to not torment ourselves with some kind of evil fear, nor will we pollute ourselves with an immoral compliance.

We are accustomed to saying, "I'll give anything for a quiet life." However, perhaps it's better said, "I'll give anything for a quiet conscience," which is best found and secured under the shield of a meek and quiet spirit. This meek spirit does not return "reviling for reviling,"[195] nor does it aggravate an already tense situation, nor does it present itself as strong and powerful. Instead, the meek spirit has learned to attach the word "only" to the power and strength of its most enraged enemies. The meek spirit says, "My enemies can *only* kill the body," but then they will witness the most righteous testimony presented to them with gentleness and respect,[196] very much like our Master who, "when he suffered, he did not threaten, but continued entrusting himself to him who judges justly."[197]

Suffering saints, just like the suffering Jesus, are compared to sheep, silent before the shearer—[198] no, silent before the butcher! The meek and quiet Christian, if properly called to it, can calmly part not only with his wool, but also with his blood. He can lose not only his property, but also his life, and even then rejoice with unspeakable joy[199] and full of glory!

Enchiridion. chpt. 8. https://classics.mit.edu/Epictetus/epicench.html. Accessed June 5, 2025.

[195] 1 Peter 3:9.

[196] 1 Peter 3:15.

[197] 1 Peter 2:23.

[198] Isaiah 53:7; Romans 8:36.

[199] Hebrews 10:34.

Angry, contrary people, on the other hand, when rebuked, are likely to add additional suffering to their lives by provoking others. They might murmur and complain, lash out at others, and use profane language that goes against the laws of our holy faith[200] and the example of our Master, Jesus Christ. In doing so, they receive more hurt than benefit from their difficult experience.

Whenever we face the honour of persecution for righteousness' sake, our focus must be to not only glorify God but also to wrap our profession of faith in the strictest controls and most aggressive restraint so as not to act improperly. This is most effectively accomplished by meekness and mildness. Doing so will reveal that we are truly under the power and influence of our holy faith, a faith which is so precious to us that we believe it is something for which it is worth our while to suffer.

e. Meekness Makes Us Fit for Death and Eternity

The grave is a quiet place.

Even the wicked "cease from troubling" in the grave.[201] Those who caused the most trouble here in this life are bound in that place to peace, and there "their hate and their envy" perish.[202]

Whether we want to or not, in the grave we will lie still and remain quiet.[203] For those, then, who are not quiet in this life, who are angry and argumentative, this will be a horrible shock as they face a sudden, forced rest after such a violent, fast-paced life!

---

[200] Ephesians 4:29.
[201] Job 3:17.
[202] Ecclesiastes 9:6.
[203] Job 3:13.

It is therefore wise for us to prepare our hearts for the grave by adapting and accommodating ourselves to that which is likely to be our new home for a long time. This act of preparation is part of what it means to die daily,[204] quieting our hearts, knowing death will soon force it upon us.

At death, the meek and quiet soul is welcomed into that very rest that it has been working towards, and how welcome is that rest to the one who worked so hard! Thoughts of death and the grave are very pleasing to those who love to be quiet, for at that time and in that place they will enter into peace and "rest in their beds."[205]

After death, we expect to face the judgement, and because of this, that day is dreadful for those who are contentious.[206] The return of the Master brings terror for those who beat their fellow servants,[207] but those who are meek and quiet are likely to have their defense already put together and their accounts paid. When this day comes, it will not be a surprise to them.

To those whose reasonableness is known to everyone, they will not be upset to hear the news that "the Lord is at hand."[208] Because of this, it is declared that we should give constant attention that, whenever our Master appears, we may be found by him to be at peace,"[209] that is, in a peaceful state in our hearts. Blessed is that servant whom, when the Lord returns, he will find him in such a state!

> A good man would hate to be taken out of this world in the middle of a heated argument with a wicked enemy. In fact, he would be horrified to find himself suddenly moving from that angry state to the calm, peaceful land of the

---

[204] 1 Corinthians 15:31.
[205] Isaiah 57:2.
[206] Romans 2:8 KJV.
[207] Luke 12:45-46.
[208] Philippians 4:5.
[209] 2 Peter 3:14.

blessed, a place where nothing but perfect love
and good-will reigns forever.[210]

Heaven is a quiet place, and no one is fit to be there except
for quiet people. The heavenly Canaan, the land of peace,
would not be heaven for those who love war. Those who are
disruptive and loud would be out of their element in that calm
place, just like a fish out of water.

The sheep of Christ, those who are patient and
inoffensive, are called to inherit the kingdom, while those who
are outside are the dogs who bite and devour.[211] David would
not fly on the wings of a hawk or eagle, but the wings of a
dove—those were the sort of wings he would use to fly away
to his desired rest.[212]

Now, my friends, put this all together and consider
whether there is any real excellence and value in a meek and
quiet spirit. It is something for all those who love God, love
their own lives, or have any realistic desire for their own
comfort, either in this world or in that which is to come.

---

[210] Archbishop Tillotson, *Family Religion*, preface. Original: *A good man
would be loath to be taken out of the world reeking hot from a sharp contention with a
perverse adversary; and not a little out of countenance to find himself in this temper
translated into the calm and peaceable regions of the blessed, where nothing but perfect
charity and good-will reigns for ever.* https://quod.lib.umich.edu
/e/eebo/A62640.0001.001/1:3?rgn=div1;view=fulltext. Accessed May 1,
2025.

[211] Revelation 22:15.
[212] Psalm 55:6.

III

Grief over Our Lack of Meekness

APPLICATION

Do we now have reason to mourn the lack of a meek and quiet spirit among those who profess faith in Christ? And do we have even more reason to mourn the lack of it within our own hearts? If this, what we see around us, is Christianity, we see how little meekness there is even among those who make great displays of their commitment to the name of Christ!

"Either this is not the gospel, or these are not followers of the gospel."[1] Oh how naked and ugly this profession of faith is when it is lacking the clothes of meekness!

When the Israelites stripped themselves of their ornaments to make the golden calf, it is said they were made naked to their shame.[2] How naked are we—like Adam when he had sinned—without this adornment of meekness? However, if this nakedness leads us to the shame of true repentance, then it is good for us!

Now, I'm not teaching you to judge and evaluate others in this matter—there is too much of that kind of thing found among Christians! We are quick to find fault in others, those to whom we should give the benefit of the doubt when we see their extreme emotions. However, we do have reason to not only condemn ourselves, but also to confess personal guilt in this matter. We sin in so many ways, and perhaps we sin in the area of meekness as much as in others, falling short of the law of meekness and quietness.

We are called Christians, and it is certainly a privilege and honour to be called by such a name! We claim the name of the meek and lowly Jesus, but how few of us are truly moved by his Spirit or conform to his example! It is a shame that those of us who profess Christ—those who are often so strict and sober in our Christ-like living—can be accused of a lack of meekness and so easily be found to be at fault. It is also a shame that those of us who pretend we are moral and devoted should live such a stubborn, uncontrolled, and sour-tempered lifestyle. This is to the great disgrace of that worthy name by which we are called.

---

[1] *Aut hoc non Evangelium, aut hi non Evangelici.* SPR Note: This may be a quote by a 15th/16th century physician and humanist by the name of Thomas Linacre, but it was a common concept/argument at the time.

[2] Exodus 32:25 KJV.

May we never say, as the Muslim man did when a Christian prince treacherously broke an alliance with him, "Oh Jesus, are these Christians?"[3]

It is clearly the design of our holy and wonderful faith to smooth, soften, and sweeten our temper. Is it not terrible that those who profess Christ should be sour and filled with bitterness, and less capable of living among and fitting in with human society than others?

It is clearly the design of our holy and wonderful faith to smooth, soften, and sweeten our temper.

There was a man who was considered a very good man in his day, and not without cause, although he had such an unhappy temper and was sometimes so moved with extreme emotions that his friend would say, "He had enough grace for ten men, but not enough for himself."[4]

The disciples of Jesus did not know "what manner of spirit" they were of.[5] We are so quick to deceive ourselves,

---

[3] SPR Note: This quote does not appear to have a definite source in writings of the time, but it may have been a commonly told story. Writers of the time often used Muslim/Christian interactions to lay out the contrast between the love and humility Christians are called to and the lifestyles actual Christians led. I suspect this approach was especially potent at that time as the world had just recently witnessed hundreds of years of Muslim (the Ottoman Empire) conflicts and conquests throughout eastern Europe. In addition to this, what is now known as western Ukraine had just recently been conquered (1672) by the Ottoman Empire.

[4] SPR Note: There does not appear to be a reference for this quote given anywhere that I could find.

[5] Luke 9:55 KJV.

especially when the experience of wandering away from Christian meekness shrouds itself under the beautiful and realistic sounding pretences of zeal for God and faith.

However, the fault of tempers and a lack of meekness is not in the profession of faith or in the strictness and commitment shown in praiseworthy Christian living, nor should we think the worse of Christianity for these blemishes. We know very well that the wisdom from above is peaceable, gentle, and open to reason,[6] and it is all sweet, pleasing, and endearing. Even so, not everyone who follows this wisdom truly lives by her ways.[7]

Instead, the fault and blame must be laid upon the corruption and foolishness of those who profess to follow wisdom, on those who are not a good image of a true Christian as they should be. They neglect the adornment of meekness, they throw away their honour, and they allow the power of the grace given to them to be trampled upon. They allow fire to go out from the stem of their shoots, and it consumes their fruit. Because of this, there is no meekness that can function as a strong stem, as a scepter to rule in their soul. "This is a lamentation and has become a lamentation."[8]

This is something similar to the terrible falling of the angels who sinned, of whom we read about in Jude 6. They did not stay within their own position of authority;[9] they lost the command they should have had over their weaker affections[10] and allowed those inferior affections to gain control. Is it not the same with those who pretend to hold such a high Christian

---

[6] James 3:17.

[7] Matthew 11:19; Luke 7:35.

[8] Ezekiel 19:14.

[9] *They kept not* την εαυτων αρχη, *Suum Principatum*. Transl: *Their own principality*. R. Cudworth. *The True Intellectual System of the Universe*. p. 816. https://quod.lib.umich.edu/e/eebo/A35345.0001.001/1:6.5?rgn=div2&view=fulltext. Accessed May 5, 2025.

[10] Original: *faculties*.

status, yet have lost control over their Christian profession, having no rule over their own spirits?[11]

And yet, praise be to God, even in this corrupt and degenerate world there are many who step forward wearing the beautiful adornment of a meek and quiet spirit. Even some whose natural temperament is hasty and grumpy have been enabled by the power of divine grace to show through their good lifestyle their works with meekness and wisdom. Truthfully, it is not as impractical as some think to overcome these extreme emotions and to preserve the peace of the soul, even on a stormy day!

But so that we may all judge ourselves and find opportunities for repentance within our hearts, I wish to mention specific examples of improper behaviour that show up as we relate with those around us. These examples give proof for the lack of meekness and quietness of spirit, and I will approach it by addressing three positions we often hold in life: positions of authority, positions under authority, and positions of equal status with those around us.

1. Those in Positions of Authority

Those in positions of authority are often quick to scold others, and this is because of a lack of meekness. It is said of him who is the great ruler of this perverse and rebellious world that "he will not always chide."[12] But, how many *lesser* rulers are there of families and of small groups of people, *little* rulers who are very much unlike God in this matter, for they are always chiding others?

Every little fault or failure of those under their authority ignites their wrath and moves them beyond self-control of

---

[11] SPR Note: Not all original versions include this paragraph.
[12] Psalm 103:9.

their anger. They are easily provoked, either for no reason at all or over very small issues. They become extremely angry, outraged, and quite unreasonable when they are provoked. The way they carry themselves through life is as a fiery person, quick to wrath. Their language becomes obscene and improper, and they don't care what they say, what they do, or who they insult. They are such worthless men that "one cannot speak to" them.[13] You would be better off meeting a bear robbed of her cubs[14] as meet this kind of person.

These people require meekness. Husbands should not be harsh with their wives.[15] Parents should not provoke their children.[16] Those in authority should not threaten.[17]

These are the rules, but how few follow them?

The wicked and uncontrolled emotions of those in authority are often justified by the excuse of necessary strictness, the maintaining of authority, and the education and control of children or those under authority, but certainly every little failure does not need to be pointed out and criticised. Perhaps many of these failures should instead be overlooked. And if the fault must be addressed and corrected, can it not be done without so much yelling and shouting?

Is this yelling the product of your meek and quiet spirit? Is this the best badge you own that proves your authority? And are these reactions the best symbols of your honour? Is there no other way of making those under your authority know their place aside from lining them up next to the dogs of your flock and threatening them like they themselves are dogs as well?

It is not that I am against proper rule and leadership within families. Sometimes a scolding is necessary to the support and preservation of the family order. Certainly there

---

[13] 1 Samuel 25:17.
[14] Proverbs 17:12.
[15] Colossians 3:19.
[16] Ephesians 6:4.
[17] Ephesians 6:9.

are times those within the family need this approach, but while you are offering leadership to others, learn to lead yourself! Do not disorder your own soul under the pretence of keeping order within your family.

For though you may not be aware of it, it is obvious that through the way you display your displeasure, doing so in ways that transgress the laws of meekness, you make yourself despicable and ridiculous. In doing so, you destroy rather than preserve your authority.

While your children may not tell you this, they may reach a point where they are unable to see you as anything other than someone who is unfit to control yourself.[18] There was a day when you yourself were nothing more than a child or a student—and perhaps even a servant or apprentice—and so if you spend even a moment in reflection, you will find you will remember the heart of a sojourner.[19] As a result, you should now treat those who serve under you just as you yourself wished to be treated back in those days.

When the time comes for you to properly express your displeasure to those under your authority—a moment necessary to address what has gone wrong—you should speak and act with meekness and quietness. In doing so, your serious and focused approach with go a long ways towards maintaining your authority, and it will command great respect, far more than yelling or an angry shouting.

Those who lead in their family and those who lead students, in this same way need to behave themselves with wisdom. In this way they will be able to avoid the two

---

[18] *Nemo egere potest nisi qui & regi. No one is fit to rule except he is willing to be governed.* Seneca the Younger https://standardbooks.org/ebooks/seneca/dialogues/aubrey-stewart/text/on-anger. Accessed May 5, 2025.
[19] Exodus 23:9.

extremes. On the one hand, they can avoid Eli's foolish indulgence[20] and on the other, Saul's violent rage.[21]

And for us, to attain this golden balance between the two, we find that wisdom is profitable to give the necessary direction.

2. Those in Positions Under Authority

Those in positions under authority are often very quick to complain. If everything is not exactly how they want it, they worry, stress, grow angry, and find themselves dissatisfied with their positions, finding fault with everything said or done to them.

This is what happens when they lack a quiet spirit, the very thing that would reconcile our hearts to our current position or job along with the difficulties and challenges we face in our workplace. This quiet spirit would also assist us in making the best of the situation, regardless of how many inconveniences come with it.

In the book of Jude, the apostle compares unquiet people to "wild waves of the sea" and "wandering stars."[22] They are grumblers and malcontents,[23] blamers of their lot,[24] as the Word says. It is an indication of an unquiet spirit to be continually complaining about our circumstances. Those wives who covered "the Lord's altar with tears"[25] wanted a meek and quiet spirit, although they did not offer tears of repentance for

---

[20] 1 Samuel 2:23-24.

[21] 2 Samuel 20:30, 33.

[22] Jude 1:13.

[23] Jude 1:16.

[24] SPR Note: This appears to be understood as a reference to Proverbs 16:33, "The lot is cast into the lap, but its every decision is from the Lord."

[25] Malachi 2:13.

sin, but tears of anguish at the disappointment they felt over their situation.

Hannah's meek and quiet spirit was in some degree lacking when she worried and wept and would not eat,[26] but prayer calmed her spirit, and her face was no longer sad.[27] For the older brother in the Parable of the Prodigal Son, his unquiet spirit fought unreasonably with his father over the matter of welcoming and entertaining the repentant prodigal.[28] Those who cannot relax will never lack something to complain about.

Even though it is hard to comprehend, the sulky, complaining, and deep worries of children and servants are just as terrible a breaking of the law of meekness as the more open, loud, and obvious passions of their parents and masters. We find the king's close servants angry with king. [29] Cain's argument with God for accepting Abel was interpreted by God as anger: "Why are you angry, and why has your face fallen?"[30] The sour looks of those under authority are a definite indication of anger deep in the heart, just as the disdainful looks of those in positions of authority are indications of their anger.

How many instances have there been in our lives of discontentment, especially under the various pressures and struggles of life? Our own consciences might answer that question.

The lack of meekness of those whom God's will has placed under the authority of others turns them into worthless men,[31] that is, those who are discontent with their position.

---

[26] 1 Samuel 1:7.
[27] 1 Samuel 1:18.
[28] Luke 15:19-32.
[29] Esther 2:21.
[30] Genesis 4:6.
[31] 1 Kings 21:13.

3. Those in Positions of Equal Status with Others

In a situation where we are of equal status, such as with fellow employees, neighbours, and with siblings, people are often very quick to clash and argue.

In the church, there are many arguments due to a lack of meekness, often over unimportant details of words and involving ridiculous disagreements. Within government and politics, there are factions and different parties driven by anger and animosity. Within neighbourhoods, there are arguments and fights and terrible lawsuits along with separation, estrangements, and awkward avoidances of one another. Even within families, envy and arguments among children and servants happens all too often as they fight, undermine, and find fault with one another.

As a result, brethren that should dwell together in unity,[32] simply do not.

Because of our lack of meekness, we react poorly to anyone who disagrees with our opinions, desires, and plans, leaving us demanding that we have our own say, whether it is right or wrong, and everything that happens must happen our own way. This lack of meekness also affects our relationship with anyone we perceive as being in competition with us, and because of this we refuse to share the spotlight with anyone or share the honour and glory that we so desperately crave for ourselves.

Our lack of meekness also shows itself in our hearts as we despise any form of contempt shown towards us, and as we are so quick to grab hold and resent the slightest insult. We are so quick to believe we have been wronged, even when there really isn't anything there, or at least nothing intended.

---

[32] Psalm 133:1.

It is not just the loud and vocal arguments that show a lack of meekness, but also those silent ones where we hold back affection and relationship. Those responses make so much less noise than the others. Those fabricated hurts and prejudices, the ones that are so shameful we won't even speak them aloud, these show how upset the spirit within us has become, lacking the adornment of meekness.

Simply put, intentionally doing anything that upsets others such as slandering, backbiting, telling secrets, gossiping, etc. is an obvious indication that we are not ready to have a quiet spirit.

So, should we not stop right now and consider our own failing in this area? Instead of condemning others, though they are certainly not perfect, should we not grieve before the Lord that we have been so unaffected by this excellent spirit of meekness? Should we not repent of all we have said or done that is contrary to the law of meekness? Instead of trying to downplay or excuse our sinful passions, it would be better to highlight them and take full responsibility for our own sin on our shoulders. "I was brutish and ignorant; I was like a beast toward you," [33] the Psalmist says as he recovers from uncontrolled anger.

Think of how often we have stood before God and before the world without this adornment of meekness, without our proper clothing, and all this to our shame!

In Scripture we see that God kept an account of all the many times Israel showed a lack of meekness. They "have put me to the test these ten times."[34] Our conscience is God's record book that keeps track of all our failings. Even what we say and do quickly is not done so quickly that God does not see. So let us often open that book now for our conviction and for our humbling, or else it will be opened one day soon by

---

[33] Psalm 73:22.
[34] Numbers 14:22.

someone else for our shame and condemnation. "If we judged ourselves truly, we would not be judged"[35] by the Lord.

We don't want to have to say, as Joseph's brothers did, "In truth we are guilty concerning our brother,"[36] although perhaps some might be called to say this for the sake of humility.

There was a time, back when I was with certain people, in a certain circumstance, that I lacked meekness. My spirit was angered, and I spoke foolishly, and now I live with this shame. I have lived a life of unquietness in my family, among my neighbours, with my anger burning, and like an immature man,[37] I have hollered out threats. By doing so, I have dishonoured my God, discredited my profession of faith, upset the quietness of my soul, grieved the blessed Spirit, and led many to sin.

For all of this, should I not be humbled and ashamed?

Before we can put on the beautiful adornment of a meek and quiet spirit, we must wash ourselves in true repentance, not only for our extreme, visible sins of angry passion, but for all the times we have neglected and omitted the duties of meekness.

---

[35] 1 Corinthians 11:31.

[36] Genesis 42:21.

[37] Original, *as in my element*. SPR Note: Element can refer not only to a basic form, but also archaically as referring to the four fundamental substances the world was believed to be composed of (earth, air, fire, and water). With this in mind along with a consideration of the context, I reworded it in the sense of maturity (the basic forms = immaturity).

IV

Scriptural Precepts

Since obtaining this goal of meekness is such a virtue and worthy of such praise, we have great reason, then, to work hard and seek it. Therefore, should we not put everything we have into acquiring this adornment of a meek and quiet spirit?

To offer a bit of direction to you in this endeavour, if you are willing to hear it, I will briefly lay out the rest of this book, focusing on the following topics:

1. Scriptural Precepts for Meekness
2. Scriptural Patterns of Meekness
3. Examples of Times when Meekness Is Especially Required
4. Some Principles to Apply to Our Lives
5. Disciplines to Apply to Our Lives

Over the course of the rest of the chapters in this book, including this one, our focus will be to work through these topics, hoping to grow in this grace of meekness. Now, as we dive into these matters, we will endeavour to hold true to the law and to the testimony.

If we set the Word of God before us as our rule and also allow ourselves to be ruled by it, we will see that God's command for us to be meek is both an adornment and a duty. And so, we will dive into the Scriptural Precepts for meekness as it is laid out in the Word of God where we are told that to seek meekness is the will of God for us.

1. Seek Meekness

In Zephaniah 2:3, we have the following command directed especially to the meek: "Seek ye the Lord, all ye meek of the earth... seek meekness."[1] Though the people were already meek—and God Himself, the One who searches the heart, pronounced them as such—even so, they needed to seek meekness. This teaches us that even those who have a great deal of this grace,[2] still need more and must desire and seek it.[3]

If someone settles down, content with the grace he has received, and does not press forward towards perfection, if he does not strive to grow in grace and to strengthen and confirm the pattern of it, nor does he strive to ignite and invigorate the working out of it in his life, we really should fear that he has no true grace at all! If this is so, this man, though his opinion of himself sits so high in his mind, he will, in the end, sit down far short of heaven.

Wherever there is life, one way or another there will be growth, and this is true until we reach the point of spiritual

---

[1] KJV.

[2] *Puto multos potuisse ad sapientiam pervenire, nisi putassent se pervenisse.* Sen. de tranqu. Transl: *I fancy that many men would have arrived at wisdom if they had not fancied that they had already arrived.* Seneca, On Tranquility of the Mind, https://trisagionseraph.tripod.com/Texts/Tranquility.html. Accessed May 8, 2025.

[3] *Si dixisti, suf lficit, periisti.* Transl. *If you said, 'Enough,' you are lost.*

maturity.[4] "He who has clean hands grows stronger and stronger."[5]

Paul was a man who had a great deal of grace, and yet we find him "forgetting what lies behind and straining forward to what lies ahead."[6] Those who joyfully accepted the plundering of their property were still told they had "need of endurance."[7]

Therefore, the meek of the earth—those who, while on the earth, are in a state of sickness and imperfection, a state of trial and temptation—still have need of meekness. They must learn to be even more calm and composed, more steady, even, and consistent in the rule of their emotions and in the management of their entire lifestyle. Those who have silenced all their angry words must learn to suppress the first rise and motions of those angry thoughts.

It is easy to see that when the meek of the earth are really concerned about seeking meekness, even when the decree is ready to bring forth,[8] when the day of the Lord's anger is quickly approaching,[9] when the times are bad, and terrible judgements are breaking in, that is the time when we need all the meekness we have and all we can get. And whatever we have will never be quite enough as we show meekness towards God (the author of our trouble) and men (the instruments of our trouble), living out our meekness as we bear the trial and hold to our testimony amidst the trial.

There is sometimes an "hour of trial,"[10] a critical day when the living out of meekness is the work of that day. Sometimes the children of men are a little extra annoying, and it is in these

---

[4] Ephesians 4:13.

[5] Job 17:9.

[6] Philippians 3:13-14.

[7] Hebrews 10:34, 36.

[8] SPR Note: The phrase, *even when the decree is ready to bring forth*, is not in all versions. I suspect this is because it is mildly bizarre and confusing. Poss. Scripture reference: Zephaniah 1:2.

[9] Zephaniah 1:14.

[10] Revelation 3:10.

times that the children of God have a little extra need of meekness. When God is *justly* angry and men are *unjustly* angry, when our mother's children are angry with us along with our father as well, when there is more than enough anger growing and building around us, then, "blessed are the meek,"[11] those who are careful to keep hold of their souls when they can keep hold of nothing else.

The way God tells us to gain meekness is to seek it. Ask God for it; pray for it! It is a fruit of the Spirit;[12] it is given by the God of all grace; and to him we must go if we desire to receive it. It is a branch of wisdom in which the one who lacks it must ask of God, and it will be given to him.[13]

The God we pray to is called "the God of endurance and encouragement,"[14] and he is the God of encouragement because he is the God of patience—for the more patient we are, the more we are comforted amidst our afflictions. Now, because he is the God of patience, we must look to him when we come to him for grace and to make us like-minded with one another,[15] that is, to make us meek and loving towards each another. For us to be meek and loving in this way is the apostle's mission as he kneels before the throne of grace.

God's people are (and should be) a generation of seekers who "earnestly desire the higher gifts"[16] and make their request to the best giver, the One who never said to the wrestling descendants of Jacob that they will seek in vain.[17] Instead, he has given us an assurance that is a firm enough foundation for us to build upon and rich enough to encourage ourselves with the words, "Seek, and you will find."[18]

---

[11] Matthew 5:5.
[12] Galatians 5:22-23.
[13] James 1:5.
[14] Romans 15:5.
[15] Philippians 2:2.
[16] 1 Corinthians 12:31.
[17] Isaiah 45:19.
[18] Matthew 7:7.

What else could we desire? Seek meekness, and you *will* find it!

The promise given is very encouraging to the meek of the earth and those who seek it: "Perhaps you may be hidden on the day of the anger of the Lord."[19] Now, though it is a promise with a *you may*, it still offers a great deal of comfort. God's probabilities are better than the world's certainties.

God's probabilities are better than the world's certainties.

The meek of the earth who hope in God's mercy and can risk everything they have on a hint of his goodness will find, to their comfort, that when God brings a flood upon the world of the ungodly, he will have an ark for all his *Noahs*. That ark of salvation is for his resting, quiet people, and in that ark, it may be that they will be hid safely away from the calamity that has come—at least, from the sting and pain of it.

They will be "hid," as Martin Luther said, "either in heaven or under heaven,"[20] either in the *possession* of heaven or under the *protection* of heaven.

---

[19] Zephaniah 2:3.

[20] Psalm 91:2. SPR Note: The quote above comes from Luther's trial under Cardinal Cajetan in Augsburg, Germany on October 8, 1518. The cardinal demanded Luther recant his beliefs and abstain from publishing "new and dangerous doctrines." Luther refused, of course, and eventually the Cardinal asked, "What do you mean? Do you rely on the force of arms? When the just punishment, and the thunder of the pope's indignation break in upon you, where do you think to remain?" Luther answered, "Either in Heaven, or under Heaven" declaring that he knew he would either be still alive (under heaven) or he would be with Christ (in heaven). Notes about this conversation can be accessed here:

2. Put on Meekness

As God's holy, beloved, chosen one, put on meekness.[21] Meekness is one of the parts of the new man which, according to the obligations we fall under due to our baptism,[22] we must put on. Put it on as armour to keep the provocations from the heart and so defend the body.[23] Those who have done this will say it is reliable armour, and when you are putting on the whole armour of God, do not forget this truth.

Put it on as your outfit, your necessary clothing which you cannot go without. Consider yourself undressed and unblessed without it. Put it on as if it is your servant's uniform by which you might identify yourself to others as the disciples of the meek, humble, and patient Jesus, and that you belong to his peaceful family.

Put on meekness as an adornment, as a robe and crown by which you may be both beautiful and dignified in the eyes of others. Put on meekness as the chosen of God,[24] holy and loved, because you *are* holy and loved in your profession of faith, and put on this meekness so that you may show yourselves to be meek in truth and reality. Be clothed with meekness as the elect of God, a choice people, a chosen people, whom God has set apart for himself from the rest of the world as holy, sanctified to God—sanctified by him!

Study these graces which put a certain glory on holiness and call those who do not have these graces to seek them as

---

https://www.monergism.com/selection-most-celebrated-sermons-martin-luther-ebook. Accessed May 14, 2025.

[21] Colossians 3:12.

[22] The phrase *which according to the obligations we fall under due to our baptism* (rewritten) is not in all versions.

[23] Original: *vitals.*

[24] *Aliter induuntur milites, aliter sacerdotes, argoinduite vobis convenientia vestimenta.* Aquin. in loc. Transl: *Some things are appropriate for soldiers, other things for priests. Put on then what is appropriate for yourself.* Thomas Aquinas, Commentary on the Epistle to the Colossians, 158. https://isidore.co/aquinas/SSColossians.htm. Accessed May 12, 2025.

those loved: loved by God, loved by man, and loved by those in positions of authority.[25] For love's sake, put on meekness!

What a winning, persuasive rhetoric! You would think this is enough to smooth the roughest soul and to soften and sweeten the most stubborn of hearts! Meekness is a grace produced by the Spirit's work in your life, a garment prepared by him. But we must put it on. In other words, we must submit our souls under the commanding power and influence of meekness.

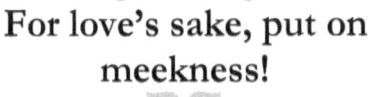

For love's sake, put on meekness!

Put it on! Not as a loosely hanging coat to be taken off when the temperature rises, but let it cling to you as a belt tightened around your waist. Put it on in a way that causes you to think of yourself as naked and ashamed without it.

3. Follow after Meekness

We are commanded in Scripture to follow after meekness, but we see that meekness, along with everything else in the list, is in there in contrast to the foolish and harmful lusts that Timothy must flee from. "O man of God, flee these things. Pursue righteousness, godliness, faith, love, steadfastness, gentleness" (*meekness* KJV).[26]

See what kind of company meekness holds in this verse! Every Christian is in a sense a man of God—though Timothy

---

[25] SPR Note: Original *ministers* which could point to those who are in authority such as civic leaders, but it can also point to those who serve you (servants). I felt the former fit the context better.

[26] 1 Timothy 6:11.

is called this as a pastor. Those who belong to God are concerned to be that man of God, to show themselves to be that man to God, and to show a life of faithful living[27] to the world. Therefore, let the men of God follow after meekness!

When anger arises and inflames our hearts, it often pushes meekness far from us, and we have to seek it when it is needed most. But we must not only seek it, but also *follow after it* and not give up our pursuit of meekness no matter what threatens to knock us off course! While others are ingenious and diligent in their pursuit of malice and revenge, pushing and carrying out their angry plans, we need to be wise and diligent to preserve the peace both at home and abroad.[28]

If others start a fire, that is their choice, but let us never be tinder for their fire.

Following meekness declares a sincere desire and serious intention to gain control of our angry passions and to check, govern, and moderate all the actions of it. Though we will never fully gain control, we must still follow after meekness and set our sights on attaining it.

Follow meekness. That is, "so far as it depends on you, live peaceably with all,"[29] endeavouring "to maintain the unity of the Spirit."[30]

We can only do our part. If others want to fight, we must still remain peaceful. If others start a fire, that is their choice.

---

[27] Original: *religion.*
[28] Original: *both within doors and without.*
[29] Romans 12:18.
[30] Ephesians 4:3.

That action is their doing, not ours, but let us never be tinder for their fire.

4. Show Meekness to Others

This is one of the subjects that Paul calls Titus to preach on: remind them to show meekness to all people.[31] This is something we need to be reminded of often. Meekness is, in this passage, in contrast to quarreling, which is the fruit and result of our own anger. It is also the cause and provocation of anger in others.

Take note of this: in this passage, we are looking at *all* meekness. That means we are told to show all kinds of meekness:

> A meekness in how you carry yourself.
> A meekness in your tolerating of difficulty.
> A meekness that limits your freedoms.
> A meekness of humility.
> A meekness of forgiveness.
> A meekness that endears our friends to us
> A meekness that reconciles us to our enemies.
> A meekness towards those under our authority.
> A meekness of obedience towards those over us.
> A meekness of wisdom towards everyone.

All meekness is a meekness that is present in *all* relationships, involved in *all* hurts towards us, active in *all* sorts of attacks against us, existing in *all* the various branches and aspects of *all* areas of life. In this aspect of our obedience to Christ we must be entirely saturated with meekness.

---

[31] Titus 3:1-2. SPR Note: this phrasing above is a mashup of the ESV and KJV.

To add to this, we must not only have meekness—*all* meekness—but we must show it by grabbing hold of this grace of meekness and pouring it into everything we do whenever there is the occasion to do it. This must pour forth meekness in our words, our expressions, and our actions. In everything we do that might be seen by others we must show that we have respect for the law of meekness, and that we take what we say and do when we are provoked seriously enough to apply what we believe to all these areas.

We must be entirely saturated with meekness.

We must not only have the law of love written in our hearts, but our tongues must have "the law of kindness,"[32] and in this, we see that the tree is known by its fruit.[33] This light must shine that others may see the good works and hear of them, not to glorify us, but to glorify our Father.[34] We should study so that we come across in all our interactions as gentle and peaceable, that all who see us may witness that we are of those who are the meek of the earth. We must not only be reasonable, but let our "reasonableness be known to everyone." [35] If someone is wise, let him show it in the "meekness of wisdom."[36]

What value do expensive clothes have if they are not worn? Why would a servant be given a quality uniform if not to show it for the honour of his master and the family he

---

[32] Proverbs 31:26 KJV.
[33] Luke 6:43-45.
[34] Matthew 5:16.
[35] Philippians 4:5.
[36] James 3:13.

serves? How can we say that we are meek if we do not show it?

When we show our meekness, we make our profession of faith beautiful, and we adorn the teachings of our God and Saviour. We may also have a good influence on others who cannot help but fall in love with such a beautiful grace, for this meekness is like a good perfume—in the hand of someone who uses it well, it fills the house with its scent.

Again, this meekness must be shown to all men, enemies as well as friends, those outside as well as those inside, everyone we have anything to do with at all! We must show our meekness not only to those we revere or respect, but also to those we might look down on, those who fall under our authority. The poor may indeed beg, but whatever might be the common practice among us, it is not the privilege of the rich to answer roughly.[37]

We must show our meekness "not only to the good and gentle, but also to the unjust. For this is a gracious thing."[38] Our meekness must reach out from us as far as our love—this commandment to show *all* meekness to *all* men[39] is very broad. We must show this meekness most to those with whom we spend the most time. There are some who, when they are among strangers, come across as mild and good-natured. Their behaviour among those they don't know is worthy and very polite, but in their families, they are stubborn, contrary, and malevolent, and those close to them hardly know how to speak to them.[40]

---

[37] Proverbs 18:23.

[38] 1 Peter 2:18-19.

[39] Titus 3:1-2 KJV.

[40] *Habet ubi se etiam in privato lare explicet magnus Animus.* Sen. Transl. *A great spirit has a place to express itself even in a private home.* Seneca, On Traquility of Mind, https://trisagionseraph.tripod.com/Texts/Tranquility.html. Accessed May 13, 2025. SPR Note: This description is very similar to the character of Talkative in Pilgrim's Progress by John Bunyan, written right around the same time.

Acting one way in private and another in public shows that the fear of man causes more restraint to their anger than the fear of God. The commandment we follow is to be meek towards all, even to the irrational animals, over whom we rule. Of course, we do not rule them as tyrants,[41] for "whoever is righteous has regard for the life of his beast."[42]

Consider the reason the apostle gives for why we should show all meekness towards all people: "For we ourselves were once foolish."[43] There was a time when we were perhaps as bad as the worst of those with whom we are now angry.[44] If we live differently now, if we are better people, we are indebted to the free grace of God in Christ because that is what made all the difference in our lives!

Should we be harsh to our brothers and sisters, even though we have found God to be so kind to us? Has God forgiven us our great debt and has he overlooked so many of our intentional acts of sin against him? Of course! And considering this, should we go to the extreme of holding onto the hurts of what has been done against us and seeing every slip and oversight on the part of others in the worst light possible?

The great gospel argument for patience with one another and for forgiveness is that "God in Christ forgave you."[45]

It may help us to hold back our anger at those under our authority if we remember not only our former sinfulness against God in our unconverted state, bur also our former

---

[41] Original: *Our rule is to be meek towards all, even to the brute creation, over whom we are lords, but must not be tyrants.*

[42] Proverbs 12:10. SPR Note: Not all versions of the original include this quote.

[43] Colossians 3:3.

[44] *Haec et nos risimus aliquando, Fiunt, non nascuntur Christiani.* Tertul. Transl. *Once these things were with us, too, the theme of ridicule… men are made, not born, Christians.* Tertullian, Apology, chpt. 18, https://www.newadvent.org/fathers/0301.htm. Accessed May 13, 2025.

[45] Ephesians 4:32; Colossians 3:13.

failings when we were younger and under the authority of others. Weren't we foolish too?

Our children are careless, playful, and disobedient, and it is nearly impossible to manage them. But... weren't we ourselves the same way when we were young? And if we have now put away childish things, they have not yet done so. Remember, it is possible to bring up children in the discipline and instruction of the Lord without provoking them to anger.[46]

5. Aspire to Be Quiet

We must aspire to be quiet,[47] that is, we must aspire not to disturb others nor to allow ourselves to be disturbed by others. Be ambitious to attain to this honour of meekness, as shown in the Word.

Most men are ambitious to attain the honour of great financial success, power, and promotion. They covet it, they seek it,[48] they plot their course across land and sea to obtain it, but the ambition of a Christian should be carried out in the pursuit of quietness. We should consider that quiet position to be the happiest position and desire it accordingly. This route lies far off the path of anger.

I cannot avoid mentioning, for the purpose of illustrating this point, the most beautiful poem by my Lord Hale, the sense of which is borrowed from a nonbeliever in Christ.

> Let him that will, ascend the tottering seat
> Of courtly grandeur, and become as great
> As are his mounting wishes: as for me,
> Let sweet repose and rest my portion be...
> ...let my age
> Slide gently by, not overthwart the stage

---

[46] Ephesians 6:4.

[47] 1 Thessalonians 4:11. SPR Note: The original uses the title, *"We must study to be quiet,"* based on the KJV.

[48] Original: *court it.*

> Of public action, unheard, unseen,
> And unconcerned, as if I ne'er had been.[49]

This is how you aspire to be quiet: subdue and keep under control all those disorderly passions which tend to disturb and cloud the soul. Also prepare yourself for this holy rest, putting yourself in a posture that invites this blessed sleep which God gives to his beloved.[50] Put great effort, as students in the arts and sciences do, into understanding the mystery of this great grace. I call it a mystery because St. Paul, who was so well versed in the deep things of God, also calls it a mystery. "I know," the mystery/secret "of facing plenty and hunger, abundance and need."[51]

This is, simply put, what it is to be quiet.

To aspire to the art of quietness is to put great effort to have in our hearts the principles, rules, and laws of meekness and to equip ourselves with all that we need to quiet the spirit during the greatest provocations. There are those who aspire to upset us, and therefore we have an even greater need to aspire for ways to quiet our hearts by careful effort so we can watch out for all that might upset or agitate us.

Christians should, above all other aspirations, aspire to be quiet, working hard[52] so that they move forward in life by an even, calm spirit, despite all the unevenness thrown at us. We must remember that good word Sir William Temple tells us. Temple heard the Prince of Orange[53] say he had heard from

---

[49] Lord Matthew Hale translated this from Seneca the Younger's *Thyestes* (Act II). https://allpoetry.com/Matthew-Hale. Accessed June 23, 2025.

[50] Psalm 127:2.

[51] Philippians 4:12.

[52] 1 Thessalonians 4:11.

[53] SPR Note: The Prince of Orange is a title given to the heir apparent of the throne in the Netherlands. This particular Prince of Orange was K. William, William III (Dutch: Willem Henrick), 1650-1702.

the master of his ship as he called out to the steersman in the midst of a storm, "Steady, steady!"

Let the hand be steady and the heart quiet, and though our journey is rough, we may weather the storm and safely reach the harbour.

A Discourse on Meekness

V

Scriptural Patterns

Good examples often assist greatly in illustrating and enforcing good rules, making them more relevant, and showing them to be practical. In the law, precedents are of great use. If we are to be found walking in the same spirit and in the same steps as those who have gone on before us to glory, a meek and quiet spirit is the spirit by which we must be motivated, and these are the steps in which we must walk. Good and wise men walk in this manner.

Let us then move forward "in the tracks of the flock,"[1] and set ourselves on a path to follow those who through faith and patience inherit the promises. We are surrounded by a great cloud of witnesses[2] who will declare in their testimony

---

[1] Song of Solomon 1:8.
[2] Hebrews 12:1.

how peaceful meekness is, and when placed on the stand, will call us to follow this beautiful law.

But for us, we will only single out a few of these people from Scripture: Abraham, Moses, David, Paul, and, of course, our Lord Jesus Christ.

1. Abraham as a Pattern

Abraham was a pattern of meekness, and he was the father of the faithful.[3] And as he was famous for faith, he was also famous for meekness. The more faith we have towards God, the more meekness we will have towards all men.

See how meek Abraham was when there was strife between his herdsmen and Lot's? If that argument had continued, it might have turned out terribly because "the Canaanites and the Perizzites were dwelling in the land." However, it was suitably addressed by the foresight of Abraham. "Let there be no strife between you and me,"[4] said Abraham, even though he could order Lot to hold his peace. For love's sake, the Patriarch pleaded with his nephew.

Every word spoken has an air of meekness about it and feels like it seeks peace. And when the hope for the prevention of strife was found in the parting of ways, even though Lot was the younger of the two, yet Abraham, for the sake of peace, gave up his right and offered Lot the first choice.[5] And after all this took place, God graciously visited Abraham and rewarded him for his mildness and humility.[6]

---

[3] Romans 4:16-22; Galatians 3:6-9. SPR Note: Some versions include the following text after this sentence: *The Apostle here in the verse but one before the Text, proposeth Sarah for an Example to Women, particularly an Example of Meekness in an inferior Relation; she obeyed Abraham, and (in token of the respect due to a Husband) she called him Lord. Now Abraham is a Pattern of the same Grace in a Superior.*

[4] Genesis 13:7-8.

[5] Genesis 13:9.

[6] Genesis 13:14.

Another example of Abraham's meekness reveals itself when Sarah argued unreasonably about her maid, angry over what she herself had brought about. "May the wrong done to me be on you! ...May the Lord judge between you and me!" Abraham could have very well replied, "You can thank yourself for that! You brought it about!" But laying aside the immediate attack, he sticks to one of the accepted rules of the relations between Sarai and Hagar, her maid: "Behold, your servant is in your power."[7]

He did not respond to her anger with his own anger. That would have ignited a terrible fire! Instead, he answered her anger with meekness, and the result was quietness.

Yet another instance of Abraham's meekness is seen in the interactions between himself and Abimelech, his neighbour. First, he enters into a covenant of friendship with him, which he confirms with an oath. Then, later, he does not rebuke him, but reproves him for the wrong Abimelech's servants had done to him regarding a well of water.[8] This gives us this rule of meekness, "Do not break a friendship over a small matter of differences."

There are many situations like this in life, and those who tend to react poorly might argue and fight about them. But for us, "What is that between you and me?"[9]

If meekness rules in our lives, small differences can be worked through without a violation or infringement on the friendship. This is the example of that great patriarch, Abraham. The future happiness of the saints is represented in Scripture as Abraham's bosom, a quiet place. Those who hope to lie in the bosom of Abraham one day soon must walk in the steps of Abraham now as we are his children. That is, we are his children if we walk faithfully in his steps.[10] Abraham is, as

---

[7] Genesis 16:5-6.
[8] Genesis 21:22-32.
[9] Genesis 23:15.
[10] John 8:39.

Maimonides states, "the father of all who are gathered under the wings of the divine Majesty."[11]

2. Moses as a Pattern

Moses was an incredible example for us of meekness. We could say it was his master-grace[12] because in this grace more than any other he excelled. The Holy Spirit testifies about Moses in this way, "the man Moses was very meek, more than all the people who were on the face of the earth."[13]

This description of Moses's character is given of him amidst an attack from members of his own house.[14] This declares openly that his quiet and patient endurance of the matter was the greatest proof and insistence of his meekness. Those who can endure a provocation from their close relatives can put up with any provocation from anyone. The meekness of Moses, just like the patience of Job, was tested in all areas. If you are wearing tested armour, you can count on it being shot at.[15]

---

[11] SPR Note: I was unable to find a location for this reference, although I suspect this is referring to Abraham Maimonides, rather than his father Moses.

[12] Josephus Antiquities, I. 4. c. 8, *Gives this character of Moses, Affectus it semper in potestate habuit, ut omnino illis career videretur, et nomina tantum eorum ex his quae in aliis hominibus conspiceret, cognita habere. Transl. He had such a full command of his passions, as if he hardly had any such in his soul; and only knew them by their names.* Josephus Anitiquities, Book 4, chpt. 8, section 49, https://penelope.uchicago.edu/josephus/ant-4.html. Accessed May 16, 2025.

[13] Numbers 12:3.

[14] Some original versions include the following: *This Character of him comes in there in a Parenthesis, (probably inserted by the same inspired Pen, that wrote the last Chapter of Deuteronomy) upon occasion of an Affront he receiv'd from those of his own House.*

[15] Original: *Armour of proof shall be sure to be shot at.* SPR Note: *Armour of proof* is armour that has been tested and confirmed ready for battle. The original proverb at the time is: *Armor of proof is surest to be shot at.* This concept of armour of proof is referenced in John Bunyan's classic, Pilgrim's

It appears as though Moses's wife, however, was not the calmest woman as we see how angry she was over the circumcising of her son. In fact, over this issue, she even called Moses a "bridegroom of blood."[16] We do not read one word of a reply from Moses, but instead he let her have her say. When God was angry or Zipporah was angry, it was best for Moses to remain quiet. The bulk of his public service was spent "in the provocation... in the day of temptation in the wilderness."[17]

The less a man fights for himself, the more God will be honourably and faithfully engaged in fighting for that man.

And of course, as if all the rebellions and all the complaining of the people of Israel were not enough to test the meekness of Moses, his own brother and sister, no less than Miriam the prophetess and Aaron the holy one of the Lord, argued with him. They spoke against him, envied the honour he received, rebuked his marriage, and were ready to

---

Progress (see Pilgrim's Progress Original Edition compiled/edited by Shawn P. Robinson, 2025, or the *Rewalked* Edition rewritten by Shawn P. Robinson, 2025) referring to the armour he is given, and it is also found in John Trapp's commentary on Genesis 44:17 where he states: *God shoots at his servants for trial, as men shoot bullets against armour of proof, not to hurt it, but to praise it.* A Commentary on the Old and New Testaments, 1662, P. 159. http://classicchristianlibrary.com/library/trapp_john/Trapp-Bible-pt1.pdf. Accessed Sept. 3, 2025.

[16] Exodus 4:25-26.

[17] Psalm 95:8 KJV.

lead a rebellion against him![18] God heard their arguments and grew angry,[19] but Moses, though he had plenty reason to angrily resent their attack, was not affected by it at all. He took no notice of it, made no complaint to God, made no answer to them, and we do not find one word that he said until we find him praying passionately for his sister who provoked him,[20] who was, at that point, suffering under God's displeasure for the attack against Moses.

The less a man fights for himself, the more God will be honourably and faithfully engaged in fighting for that man.[21] When Christ said, "I do not seek my own glory," he quickly added, "there is One who seeks it, and he is the judge."[22] It was during the attack from his brother and sister that Moses received this commendation: "Now the man Moses was very meek, more than all people who were on the face of the earth."[23]

> No man could have given greater proofs of courage than Moses. He slew the Egyptian, beat the Midianite shepherds, confronted Pharaoh in his own court, not fearing the wrath of the king; he durst look God in the face amid all the terrors of Mount Sinai, and draw near to the thick darkness where God was; and yet that Spirit which made and knew his heart, saith he was the meekest, mildest man upon the earth. Mildness and fortitude may well lodge together in the same breast, which corrects the mistake

---

[18] Number 12:1-2.

[19] Numbers 12:2, 9.

[20] Numbers 12:13.

[21] Original: *The less a man strives for himself, the more is God engaged in honor and faithfulness to appear for him.*

[22] John 8:50.

[23] Numbers 12:3.

of those that will allow none valiant but the fierce.[24]

The meekness of Moses qualified him to be a judge, even to be a king in Jeshurun [25] among a people so very cantankerous that they gave him the chance to use every bit of meekness he had, and all that was just barely enough to endure their attitude in the wilderness. When they murmured against him, argued with him, stood against his authority, and were at times ready to stone him, he held very little resentment towards their provocations, showing very little response or concern.

Instead of using his influence in heaven to call down plagues on the people, he made it his business to stand in the gap, and by his intercession for the people, turn away the wrath of God from them. And he did not simply do this once or twice, but many times.

However, we must observe that even though Moses was the meekest man on the earth, if God's honour and glory were concerned, no one was more passionate or upset. Consider his resentment of the golden calf when, in holy indignation at their wicked sin, he deliberately broke the tablets. [26] And when Korah and his crew tried to push their way into the priestly office, Moses, in his righteous anger said to the Lord, "Do not respect their offering."[27]

The man who was a lamb when it came to defending his own cause was a lion when it came to the cause of God. Anger at sin is very much consistent with a heart ruled by meekness.

---

[24] Bishop Joseph Hall, D.D., Contemplations on the Historical Passages of the Old and New Testaments, 1858, page 69, https://ia802300.us.archive.org/29/items/contemplationson00halluoft/c ontemplationson00halluoft.pdf. Accessed May 16, 2025.

[25] SPR Note: *Jeshurun* is a biblical word referring to the people of Israel. Deuteronomy 33:5.

[26] Exodus 32:19.

[27] Numbers 16:15.

It also cannot be forgotten that though Moses was the meekest man on the earth, he still once broke the laws of it. When he was old and his spirit was provoked, he spoke foolishly and it went poorly for him.[28] This, of course, is not written for imitation, but for admonition, not to justify our rash anger, but to call us to stand on guard at all times against that anger, that "anyone who thinks that he stands [may] take heed lest he fall,"[29] and that the one who has fallen in this way may not be surprised that he has come under the rebuke of God's power in this world as Moses did. To add to this, it is written so that those who are rebuked will not despair, thinking they have no hope for a pardon if they repent.

3. David as a Pattern

Another pattern in Scripture for us of meekness was none other than David himself, and it is promised that "the feeblest among them… shall be like David."[30] In this, as in other areas, he was a man after God's own heart.[31]

When David's own brother was rough with him for no reason at all, "Why have you come down?" David answered with mildness. "What have I done now? Was it not but a word?"[32] When his enemies tried to disgrace him, he did not allow himself to be upset by it. "I am like a deaf man; I do not hear."[33] When Saul persecuted him with such relentless malice, he did not take advantage when he had the opportunity, on more than one occasion, to take revenge. Instead, he left it to God.[34]

---

28 Psalm 106:32-33.
29 1 Corinthians 10:12.
30 Zechariah 12:8.
31 1 Samuel 13:14.
32 1 Samuel 17:28-29.
33 Psalm 38:13.
34 1 Samuel 24:1-7; 26:6-12.

David's meek spirit agreed with the proverb of the ancients, "'Out of the wicked comes wickedness.' But my hand shall not be against you."[35]

When Nabal's uncivilized rudeness angered him, Abigail's prudence quickly calmed him, and it pleased David to be calmed.[36] When Shimei cursed him[37] with a bitter curse amidst David's calamity, he did not resent the offense, nor would he entertain any talk of punishing the offender. "Leave him alone, and let him curse, for the Lord has told him to."[38] David quietly committed his cause to the Lord, the one who judges justly.[39]

There are other instances in David's story that also show the truth of his words, "I have calmed and quieted my soul like a weaned child."[40] And yet, David was a great soldier, a man of celebrated courage! He slew a lion, a bear, and a Philistine—as much a ravenous beast as either of the other two—which shows that it was his wisdom and grace, not his cowardice, that made him so quiet.

David was a man who faced many upsetting and disturbing experiences in the years of his life, and though they ruffled him a little, he still mostly maintained an admirable

---

[35] 1 Samuel 24:13.

[36] 1 Samuel 25:1-35.

[37] *Non ergo movebatur convici's David, cui abundabat bonorum operum conscientia ita{que} is qui cito injuria movetur facit se dignum contumelia videri.* Ambr. De Offic. Lib. 1. Cap. 6. Transl. *David was silent… he did not return the abuse… nor was he disturbed… for he had full knowledge of his own good works. He, then, who is quickly roused by wrong makes himself seem deserving of insult.* Ambrose, On the Duties of the Clery, Book 1, chpt. 6, 21-22. https://www.newadvent.org/fathers/34011.htm. Accessed May 16, 2024.

[38] 2 Samuel 16:10-12.

[39] 2 Samuel 16:12; 1 Peter 2:23.

[40] Psalm 131:2. *David fuit fortis in praelio, mansuetus in imperio, patiens in convitio, ferre magis promptu quam referre injurias.* Ambr. l. 2. c. 17. Transl. *David was brave in battle, gentle in ruling, patient under abuse, and more ready to bear than to return wrongs.* Ambrose, On the Duties of the Clery, Book 2, chpt. 7, 32. https://www.newadvent.org/fathers/34012.htm. Accessed May 16, 2025.

temper, an evenness and composed mind which was very much worthy of imitation.

One time when David grew afraid before Abimelech, he changed his behaviour and pretended to be insane,[41] yet even so, his mind remained so quiet and undisturbed that he was able to pen the 34th Psalm. In this Psalm, we read not only the goodness of the matter and the calmness of his expression, but he also managed to compose it alphabetically in the Hebrew. This shows how, even in that moment, in such a difficult time, he remained calm and relaxed, very much in command of his own thoughts. At another time, his own followers spoke of stoning him. Though he could not calm the storms inside the hearts of his own troops, he could calm his own spirit, and he accomplished this by strengthening "himself in the Lord his God."[42]

Now, as for the prayers against his enemies which we find in some of his psalms, they certainly did not flow from an ungodly emotion as they did not in the slightest clash with the evangelical laws of meekness. It is difficult to imagine someone who was so calm in his regular interactions with others might be so sinfully stormy in his heart with his devotions. Nor should these passages be viewed through the lens of private expressions of his own angry resentments, but rather as inspired predictions of God's judgement on the visible, stubborn enemies of Christ and his kingdom.

This can be seen by comparing Psalm 69:22-23 with Romans 11:9-10 and comparing Psalm 109:8 with Acts 1:20. These prayers are not in contrast to the spirit of the gospel, but they are similar in this way to the cries of the souls from under

---

[41] 1 Samuel 21:10-15. SPR Note: 1 Samuel 21 calls the Philistine king by his name, Achish, while Psalm 34 refers to him as Abimelech. This is due to a tradition at the time of calling kings in that region *Abimelech* which means *my father is king*, despite his name actually being Achish.

[42] 1 Samuel 30:6.

the altar [43] or the triumphs of heaven and earth in the destruction of Babylon. [44]

4. Paul as a Pattern

Though the Apostle Paul's natural temperament seems to have been intense and eager which made him exceptionally active and zealous, that temperament was so transformed and sanctified that he ended up exceptionally meek. He became "all things to all people." [45] He worked to please everyone he interacted with and to make himself engaging to them for their good, for their edification.

How patiently did he endure the greatest attacks and indignities, not only from the Jews and heathens, but from false brothers who were so creative in coming up with ways to abuse and undermine him. How glad was he that Christ was preached, even though it was out of envy and ill-will, by those who worked hard to add affliction to his imprisonment. [46]

When it came to leading the church, he was not carried along by the heat of anger, but he calmly considered the use of the rod of discipline whenever the need arose. "Shall I come to you with a rod, or with love in a spirit of gentleness?" [47] In other words, "Shall I go straight to judgement, or shall I instead continue in the same gentle manner as I have until this point, waiting for God to change your heart?"

This is where the spirit of meekness appears more open and understandable than the use of the rod of discipline, though the rod itself is also very much consistent with meekness.

---

[43] Revelation 6:10.
[44] Revelation 19:1.
[45] 1 Corinthians 9:19-23.
[46] Philippians 1:17.
[47] 1 Corinthians 4:21.

There are, of course, many other examples of meekness I could suggest, but time would fail me if I spoke of Isaac, Jacob, Joseph, Joshua, Samuel, Job, Jeremiah, all the prophets and apostles, martyrs, confessors, and eminent saints, those who by meekness subdued not kingdoms, but their own spirits. They stopped the mouths, not of lions, but of more fierce and dreaded enemies. They quenched the violence, not of fire, but of extreme and unruly passions. Through this they worked righteousness, obtained promises, escaped the edge of the sword, and out of weakness, they were made strong, and amidst all this they received their commendation.[48]

5. Our Lord Jesus

Now, our Lord Jesus was the great pattern of meekness and quietness of Spirit.

All the rest had their blemishes—even the most beautiful marble has its flaws—but in Christ we have a copy without a blot.[49] As a result, we should follow those others only so far as they were conformable to this great original. "Be imitators of me," Paul says, "as I am of Christ."[50]

Christ fulfilled all righteousness and was a complete and perfect pattern of all that is holy, just, and good. But I think that in most, if not all places in Scripture, where he is particularly and expressly given to us as an example, it is to direct us towards our Christian duties. These duties are those things which tend to sweeten our relationships with one another in Christ.

---

[48] Hebrews 11:2, 32-40.

[49] SPR Note: I kept some of the original wording here (*a copy without a blot*) despite how uncommon this analogy is for today's readers as I felt this particular phrase was far more poetic than a modern, *All the rest had their errors, but in Christ we have a document without a typo*. There seems to be something lacking in such a contemporary phrasing. Additional Note: Some originals do not have the phrase, *the fairest marbles had their flaws*.

[50] 1 Corinthians 11:1.

The Word was made flesh and dwelt among us[51] that he might teach us how to dwell together in unity.[52] We must walk in love as Christ loved us,[53] forgive as Christ forgave us,[54] please one another for Christ did not please himself,[55] be charitable to the poor for we know the grace of our Lord Jesus,[56] wash one another's feet, that is, stoop down to the humblest forms of love, for this is what Christ did,[57] and we must do all things with humility of mind for that is the same mind Christ Jesus had.[58] But even beyond what things he taught us, our Lord Jesus was an example of meekness.

Moses had this grace as a servant, but Christ had it as a Son—and he was anointed with it beyond measure! He is called the "Lamb of God"[59] for his meekness, patience, and inoffensiveness, and even in his glory he maintains the same character. One of the elders told John that "the Lion of the tribe of Judah" would open the scroll, and "I saw," wrote John, "a Lamb."[60] The One who was a Lion for strength and courage was a Lamb for mildness and gentleness.

And if a Lion, "the Lion of the tribe of Judah" which the dying patriarch describes as a lion gone up from the prey, that is "stooped down; he crouched as a lion," not to be roused.[61] This speaks of the quietness and rest of even this lion! If Christ is a Lion, he is a Lion resting, while the devil is a lion roaring.[62] However, the praises offered to Christ by the heavenly hosts speak of him as a Lamb. Blessing and honor and glory and

---

[51] John 1:14.
[52] Psalm 133:1.
[53] Ephesians 5:2.
[54] Colossians 3:13.
[55] Romans 15:2-3.
[56] 2 Corinthians 8:9; 9:7.
[57] John 13:14; Matthew 20:27-28.
[58] Philippians 2:3-5.
[59] John 1:29, 36.
[60] Revelation 5:5-6.
[61] Genesis 49:9.
[62] 1 Peter 5:8.

might to him who sits on the throne. They do not say to the Lion of the tribe of Judah, but to "the Lamb."[63]

Even though he has a name given to him above every name,[64] he will be known by the name that points to his meekness as if this were to be his name forever, his memorial to all generations. "His name is the Lord, exult before him! Father of the fatherless and protector of widows."[65] Christ rides "victoriously for the cause of truth and meekness and righteousness."[66]

It is in the character of every true saint to follow the Lamb, and as a Lamb, they follow him in his meekness.

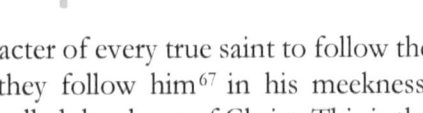

Now, it is in the character of every true saint to follow the Lamb, and as a Lamb, they follow him[67] in his meekness. Therefore, they are often called the sheep of Christ. This is the part of his example that he directly calls us to follow: "Learn

---

[63] Revelation 5:8, 12-13.

[64] Philippians 2:9.

[65] Psalm 68:4-5. SPR Note: Some versions include the following sentence here: *Some make his name Chrisos, to have an allusion to Christos, which signifies kind, and gentle, and gracious.* Additional NOTE (attached to the additional sentence mentioned here): *The Heathen by mistake, called Christ Chrestus, Gracious, and the Christians Chrestiani.* So Sueton. vit. Claud. c. 25. Impulsore Chresto. Lactantius takes notice of this, Instit. l. 4. c. 7. So doth Tertullian, and thence calls the Christian Name: *Nomen Innocuum, an innocent name.* Tertullian, Apology. https://www.newadvent.org/fathers/0301.htm. Accessed June 5, 2025.

[66] Psalm 45:4.

[67] Revelation 14:4.

from me, for I am gentle[68] and lowly in heart."[69] If the Master is mild, it does not very well fit for the servant to be argumentative.[70] This call to meekness is what the Apostle speaks of when referring to Christ's meekness amidst his sufferings, "Leaving you an example, so that you might follow in his steps."[71]

We will now take some time to examine the meekness of our Lord Jesus in three areas: *towards his Father*, *towards his friends*; and *towards his foes*. In each of these areas, he is an example to us.

a. The Meekness of Jesus towards His Father

Jesus was very meek towards God his Father, cheerfully submitting his entire will and standing firm in this submission.[72] Declaring his purpose,[73] he states, "Behold, I have come… I delight to do your will,"[74] even though it led to a very difficult life of servitude. Yet, this service was his food,[75] and he always did those things which pleased his Father.[76] In the same way in his living out of this will he acquiesced from first to last. When the day came for him to face his crucifixion, though we may be shocked at it, he said, "My Father, if it be possible, let this cup pass from me," although he quickly

---

[68] KJV *meek*.

[69] Matthew 11:29.

[70] Original: *froward*.

[71] 1 Peter 2:21.

[72] Original: *and standing complete in it*.

[73] Original: *commanding will*. Considering an older meaning of *commanding*, this would appear to point to *a priority* or *a will that stands out*.

[74] Psalm 40:6-8.

[75] John 4:34.

[76] John 8:29.

submitted with a great deal of meekness by saying, "not as I will, but as you will."[77]

Even though it was such a bitter cup to drink, his Father still put it into his hand, and therefore Jesus drank it without struggle or reluctance. And when it came to moving forward on that fateful day, he reasoned through the matter, moving from his commitment to the Lord's will to obedience.[78] "Shall I not drink the cup that the Father has given me?"[79] And in there we see the reason why he would not allow a sword drawn in his defence.[80]

b. The Meekness of Jesus towards His Friends

Jesus was very meek towards his friends, those who loved and followed him. Consider his remarkable mildness, gentleness, and tenderness with which he trained up his disciples, even though from the beginning till the end he was "a man of sorrows and acquainted with grief."[81] When a man's nature is corrupt, he tends to be evil and argumentative with others, but when it came to Christ and his disciples, he showed such meekness and calmness through the way he bore with their weaknesses and sinfulness.

After they had served long under the oversight and influence of such a teacher and had all the advantage that men can have in being acquainted with the things of God, see how weak and defective they still were in their knowledge, gifts, and graces! How ignorant and forgetful they were! How slow of

---

[77] Matthew 26:39-42.

[78] SPR Note: Some original versions do not include this sentence or the latter half of the previous sentence (from after *drank it*).

[79] John 18:11.

[80] SPR Note: Some original versions do not include this sentence.

[81] Isaiah 53:3.

heart to understand and believe! What mistakes they made! They appeared to be very poor scholars, unable to learn.[82]

But since their hearts were true to him,[83] he did not send them away nor did he turn them out of his school. Instead, he fixed their mistakes, taught them their duty and the doctrine they were to preach, precept upon precept, line upon line.[84] He taught them, as they were able to bear it,[85] and as one who considered their limits. He dealt gently "with the ignorant and wayward, since he himself is beset with weakness."[86]

As long as he was with them, he continued to put up with them.[87] This, what we see in Christ, is a great encouragement for Christian disciples,[88] and it is also a great example for Christian teachers.

Christ was also meek in his forgiving and overlooking of their unkindness and disrespect towards himself, not going to the extreme of pointing out how they had acted against him. When they complained at the cost he would have to pay and called it a waste, feeling indignant towards it, he did not resent their position as he could very well have done, nor did he seem to notice how much of what they said really reflected upon himself. He also did not condemn them in any way, other than in a round-about-way by commending the woman.[89]

When Peter, James, and John, the first three disciples, were with him in the garden, and they inappropriately slept while he was praying in his agony, they not only showed so

---

[82] Original: *Dull scholars it should seem they were, and bad proficients.*

[83] Original: *But their hearts being upright with him...* SPR Note: It appears that the best understanding of *upright* here (considering context and theology) would be to see it as a matter of genuine faith.

[84] Isaiah 28:10-13.

[85] John 16:12.

[86] Hebrews 5:2.

[87] Mark 9:19.

[88] Original: *learners.*

[89] Matthew 26:8-11.

little concern for him but they also insulted him terribly,[90] yet even so, pay attention to how meekly he spoke to them:[91] "Could you not watch with me for one hour?"[92] And when they had nothing to say for themselves, so inexcusable was their sin, he had something to say for them. "The spirit indeed is willing, but the flesh is weak."[93]

When Peter denied Jesus and had cursed and sworn that he did not know him—nothing could be unkinder than that, even aside from the falsehood and unfaithfulness of it— consider the meekness of Jesus! It is not written that the Lord turned and frowned upon Peter, though he deserved to be frowned down into hell, but "the Lord turned and looked at Peter."[94] And that look put him back on the path to heaven as it was a kind look, not an angry one.

Some days later when Christ and Peter met in Galilee, after they had dined together as a token of reconciliation as well as talked together, not a word was said of this matter. Christ did not accuse him of his sin, nor did he rebuke him for it, nor was there anything that suggested a falling out of their relationship. The only thing that happened was the renewing of their love with greater affection.[95] This teaches us to forgive and forget the unkindness of those who are, for the most part,[96] our true friends. If any occasion of disagreement arises, we should turn it into an occasion of confirming our love for them, as the Apostle expresses in 2 Corinthians 2:8.[97]

---

[90] Original: *and such a grievous slight did they put upon him.* This phrase is not in all originals.

[91] Original includes the phrase: *did not give them any hard language.*

[92] Matthew 26:40; Mark 14:37.

[93] Matthew 26:41.

[94] Luke 22:61.

[95] John 21:15-17.

[96] SPR Note: Some original versions include the phrase: *we are satisfied.*

[97] SPR Note: Some original versions end after: *confirming our love for them.*

c. The Meekness of Jesus towards His Enemies

Jesus was very meek towards his enemies, those who hated and persecuted him. In fact, the entire story of his life is filled with instances of invincible meekness. While he "endured from sinners such hostility against himself,"[98] which constantly beat against him,[99] he held a perpetual serenity and harmony within his heart and was never unsettled even a little bit by it.

When his preaching and miracles were criticized and insulted, and he himself slandered terribly, not only was he called a companion of drunkards but also someone who was in league with the devil, he bore it with such wonderful calmness! He mildly replied with such reason and tenderness when he could have replied with thunder and lightning! How satisfying, after so many jealous attacks, to declare that "wisdom is justified by her deeds."[100]

**Christianity was intended
to revive humanity and to
make those who had turned
themselves into beasts back
into human beings.**

When some of his disciples would have called fire down from heaven on those rude people who refused to welcome Jesus in their town, he was so far from complying with their

---

[98] Hebrews 12:3.

[99] Original: *which was a constant jarr.* Some original versions do not include this phrase.

[100] Matthew 11:19; 12:24.

wish that he rebuked it! "Ye know not what manner of spirit ye are of."[101] "This persuasion is not from him who calls you."[102] The intention of Christ and of his holy religion is to shape men into mild and merciful people and to make them rationally tender towards the lives and comforts of even their worst enemies. Christianity was intended to revive humanity and to make those who had turned themselves into beasts back into human beings.

However, considering all these examples, our Lord Jesus showed his meekness in a special way when he suffered at the end—that awful day! Though Jesus was the most innocent and most wonderful person who ever existed, and because of the doctrine he preached and the miracles he performed, he richly deserved all the honour and respect that the world could offer—and infinitely more. And though the injuries he received were ingeniously and industriously developed for the greatest amount of insult and upset, still he received it all with an undisturbed meekness, and with that shield, he quenched all the fiery darts shot at him by his malicious enemies.[103]

His meekness towards his enemies came out in how he spoke to them: not one angry word amidst all the indignities they threw at him! "When he was reviled, he did not revile in return."[104] When he was hit, spit upon, and abused, he took it patiently. In fact, it's a surprise to consider the gracious words which, even at that time, came out of his mouth. Witness the mild reply to the man who struck him, "If what I said is wrong, bear witness about the wrong; but if what I said it right, why do you strike me?"[105]

Also consider how his meekness towards his enemies revealed itself in how he spoke to God for them. "Father,

---

[101] Luke 9:51-56 KJV.
[102] Galatians 5:8.
[103] Ephesians 6:16.
[104] 1 Peter 2:23.
[105] John 18:23.

forgive them."[106] In this, he gave us an example of his own rule, "Pray for those who persecute you."[107] Even though he was in the middle of the most serious transaction that ever passed between heaven and earth, and though he had so much to take care of with God for himself and for his friends, he still did not forget to offer this prayer for his enemies.

The mercy he begged God for regarding them was the greatest mercy—the very mercy he was at that moment dying to purchase and bring about—the pardon for their sins. Not only "Father, *spare* them," or "Father, *give them relief*," but "Father, *forgive* them." The excuse he offered in defence for their crime was the best that could be given, "for they know not what they do."[108] They did it ignorantly.[109]

Following Christ's Example

Now, all these things our Master left us as an example. What is the practice of religion, other than for us to strive to imitate God? And what is the beginning of this faith, other than the image of God renewed within us? We are called to be followers of God as dear children, but this sets the image we are called to follow at an extreme distance,[110] for God is in heaven, and we are on earth! Therefore, in the Lord Jesus Christ—God incarnate, God present in human nature—the image is brought near, brought among us, and the image is very literally translated for us, and in that the example appears much more applicable. "Whoever has seen me," says Christ, "has seen the Father,"[111] and because of this, whoever imitates Christ, imitates the Father.

---

[106] Luke 23:34.

[107] Matthew 5:44.

[108] Luke 23:34.

[109] Acts 3:17; 1 Corinthians 2:8; 1 Timothy 1:7. SPR Note: Some original versions do not include this sentence.

[110] Original: *this sets the copy we are to write after at a mighty distance.*

[111] John 14:9.

The religion that our Lord Jesus brought into the world was to establish the peace and order of the world, being in every way brought forward for this purpose, and being designed to recover the lost souls of men from their degenerate state, to sweeten their spirits and temper, to befriend human society, and to make it conformable to the blessed society above. Jesus not only gave such rules and direction that were wonderfully effective for this great purpose, but he also gave them to the world by his own lovely and admirable example.

Are we not called *Christians* after the name of *Christ?* We call him Master and Lord, and shall we not seek to adjust our lives to imitate him? We say we rejoice in him as the One who runs before us, but shall we not run after him? For what purpose have we come under his banner, other than to follow him as our leader? We all have reason to recognise Jesus Christ's meekness, since we have all provoked him so much and so often that if he were not meek, we would all be in hell long ago!

For what purpose have we come under his banner, other than to follow him as our leader?

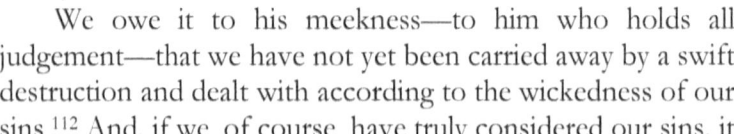

We owe it to his meekness—to him who holds all judgement—that we have not yet been carried away by a swift destruction and dealt with according to the wickedness of our sins.[112] And, if we, of course, have truly considered our sins, it stands to reason that we would be greatly humbled.[113]

---

[112] Psalm 103:10. Original: *to the desert of our sins.*

[113] Some originals: *one would think should tend greatly to soften us.* Other originals: *one would think should tend greatly to the mollifying of us.*

The Apostle pulls an argument from the kindness and love shown to us, the very kindness we, those who were foolish and disobedient, have experienced. His argument is given to persuade us to be "gentle, to show perfect courtesy toward all people." [114] He also entreated the Corinthians "by the meekness and gentleness of Christ,"[115] a thing which is very wonderful, dear, precious, and beneficial to us.

Let the same mind be in us, not only that mind which was in Christ, but as we are comforted to find, still is in Christ Jesus![116] So that we will not forfeit our share in his meekness, let us walk in the steps of it, and just as we hope to be like him one day when we are in glory, we should strive to be like him in grace, in this grace right now!

> # We all have reason to recognise Jesus Christ's meekness, since we have all provoked him so much and so often that if he were not meek, we would all be in hell long ago!

Here is a rule by which we will all be tested one day, that if anyone "does not have the spirit of Christ," that is, if his spirit is not in some measure like the spirit of Christ, he "does not belong to him."[117] And if we are not owned by Christ, we are lost forever.

---

[114] Titus 3:2.
[115] 2 Corinthians 10:1.
[116] Philippians 2:5.
[117] Romans 8:9.

A Discourse on Meekness

VI

When Meekness Is Especially Required

This rule of meekness is certainly broad (we must show all meekness[1]), so perhaps it is helpful to take a look at some special cases to which the Scripture applies this rule.

1. We Must Offer Reproofs with Meekness

We must be willing and able to reprove faults in others with a heart filled with meekness. The Apostle directs us that

---

[1] Titus 3:2 KJV.

"if anyone is caught in any transgression," that is, if he is surprised by a temptation and is overcome—something that happens to even the best of us if God leaves us to our own ways—"you who are spiritual should restore him in a spirit of gentleness."[2]

Now, who is this "spiritual" man to whom he gives this rule? Paul does not mean ministers only, as if they are the only spiritual ones, despite the fact that ministers might be the primary focus here.[3] Obviously, this is a rule to all private Christians. Everyone, if the opportunity arises, must reprove or speak to someone for the purpose of correcting their error, and when the opportunity arises, it must be done in meekness.

You who are spiritual, if you would think of yourselves that way, moved by the Holy Spirit and caring about the things of the Spirit, must be careful in this matter. Those who are the best of Christians, those who excel in grace, holiness, and the best gifts—these are those who are called spiritual as opposed to infants in Christ[4]—let them consider themselves under a personal obligation to help others. Where God gives five talents, he expects the improvement of five.[5] The strong must "bear with the failings of the weak."[6] The setting of a dislocated joint or broken bone is, for the moment, painful to the patient, but it has to be done, and it is a necessary step before the broken bones may heal and rejoice.[7]

Now, this must all be done with a spirit of meekness, with a bright innocence, a gentleness, and a display of love and kindness that is as genuine as it can be.

---

[2] Galatians 6:1.

[3] Isaiah 29:21. *Reprovers in the gate, i.e. reprovers by office.* SPR Note: the latter half of this sentence (from *as if they are the only spiritual ones*) is not in all original versions.

[4] 1 Corinthians 3:1.

[5] Matthew 25:14-30.

[6] Romans 15:1. SPR Note: Some original versions include the following phrase: *Do you therefore restore such a one, kataptidsete—set him in joint again.*

[7] Psalm 51:8. Original: *and it is in order to the making of broken bones to rejoice.*

The three qualifications of a good surgeon are essential to someone who reproves others:

1. To have an eagle's eye
2. To have a lion's heart
3. To have a lady's hand

These three qualifications point towards one who is endued with a great deal of wisdom, courage, and meekness. Though it is sometimes needed to reprove with warmth, we must never reprove with wrath, "for the anger of man does not produce the righteousness of God."[8]

There is a difference, without contradiction, between the direction Paul gives to Timothy and what he gives to Titus in this matter. To Titus, he writes, "rebuke them sharply" and to "rebuke with all authority."[9] To Timothy, he writes to not "be quarrelsome but kind to everyone," and to rebuke "with complete patience."[10]

The reason for this difference may be found in the different temper of those whom each of these men had to deal with. Timothy was among the Ephesians, a people who had a pattern of obedience to the Apostle's message,[11] a people who could be easily managed. With people like that, Timothy needed to be gentle. Titus was among the Cretans. They were headstrong[12] and could not be worked with unless sharper methods were employed.[13]

Therefore, when we reprove, a distinction must be made. With some, we must "have mercy," while with others we must

---

[8] James 1:20.

[9] Titus 1:13; 2:15.

[10] 2 Timothy 2:24; 4:2.

[11] Original: *a tractable, complaisant people.*

[12] SPR Note: Some original versions include the words *rough hewn* here implying either that they were only roughly cut out, still needing a lot of work, or that they were simply rough people.

[13] Titus 1:12.

have "mercy with fear," but we must never snatch "them out of the fire"[14] with anger.

Now, it is also possible that the reason for the different instructions they received was found in the different tempers of Timothy and Titus:[15]

> Titus was a man of a very soft and mild temper, and he needed a spur to push him to be bolder in his reproofs, but Timothy was a more hot-tempered, and he needed a bridle to keep him from an unrestrained anger in his reproofs.[16]

This teaches us that those who are naturally bold and intense should double their guard on their own spirits when they are reproving another person, so that they do it with *all meekness.*

Christ's ministers must be careful to conceal *their own* wrath when they display *God's* wrath. They must be fiercely protective of their hearts, lest sinful anger creep in and move through them under a cloak of zeal against sin. When reproving—regardless of who is the reprover—devolves into railing, reviling, and scornful language, how can we expect the desired result? Such an approach may push someone to arguments and evil works, but it will never stir anyone to love and good works.[17]

The work of heaven is not likely to be done by a tongue set on fire by hell.[18]

---

[14] Jude 1:22-23.

[15] *as Gregory, one of the ancients, assigns it.*

[16] Gregory the Great, Pastoral Rule, Book III, Chptr. 16, https://www.newadvent.org/fathers/36013.htm. Accessed May 22, 2025. SPR Note: this reference to Gregory the Great's writing is not a direct quote, but a rewrite based on both M. Henry's paraphrasing of it and the original translated work provided by New Advent.

[17] Hebrews 10:24.

[18] James 3:6.

Does Christ need madmen? Or will you speak to others with deceit and anger for Jesus? A medicine given too hot will scald the patient and do more harm than good, and in the same way, many corrections given to others, as helpful and necessary as they are, have been spoiled by an inappropriate management of the conversation.

The work of heaven is not likely to be done by a tongue set on fire by hell.

Meekness hides the scalpel, sugar-coats the pills, and makes the medicine easy to swallow. Meekness dips the nail in oil allowing it to drive into the wood all that much easier.

Twice, in Scripture, we find Jonathan reproving his father for his rage against David. Once he did it with meekness, and it turned out well.[19] "Let not the king sin against his servant David," and it is said, "Saul listened to the voice of Jonathan."[20] The second time, however, his spirit was angry when he asked, "Why should he be put to death?" and nothing good came of it. Saul was not only impatient of the reproof, but he was enraged at the reprover, even casting a javelin at him![21]

Reproofs are likely to be successful when the good will of the reprover comes clearly through, and when they are made up of soft words and hard arguments. This is to restore "in a spirit of gentleness,"[22] and there is a good reason tacked onto

---

[19] SPR Note: *and it turned out well* (Original: *and it sped well*) is not in all original versions.
[20] 1 Samuel 19:4-6.
[21] 1 Samuel 20:32-33.
[22] Galatians 6:1.

this command: "Keep watch on yourself!" "He may fall today, but I may fall tomorrow."[23] Those who think they stand fast do not know how soon they may be shaken and overthrown.[24] Because of this, we must treat those who are overtaken in a fault with the same tenderness and compassion that we would wish to find if we were the one to be caught in sin.

2. We Must Receive Rebukes with Meekness

Not only must we offer reproof with meekness, we must also receive reproofs with meekness. If we act in a way that deserves a rebuke and meet with those who are so just and kind as to give it to us, we must remain quiet under the rebuke. We should never quarrel with the reprover, nor object to the reproof, nor worry that a sore spot has been poked. Instead, we should submit to the reproof, laying our souls under the conviction of it.[25]

If a reproof is for our healing, it is only proper for us to receive it with patience. "Let a righteous man strike me—it is a kindness,"[26] a wonderful oil, healing to the wounds of sin, and making the face shine. Let us never think that it will break our head simply because it helps to break our heart. Meekness endures admonishments, taking them patiently and thankfully,

---

[23] *ille hodie, ego cras*, meaning roughly *him today, me tomorrow*, or *he fell today, I fall tomorrow*. SPR Note: This appears to be a statement derived from Bernard of Clairvaux (1090-1153), a French Abbot and theologian. While this quote does not appear to be a direct quote, it seems to come from Bernard's writings on topics such as humility.

[24] 1 Corinthians 10:12

[25] *Neque ulli patientius reprehen/dunter, quàm qui maxime laudari merentur.* Plin. Transl. *Besides, it is just those people who most deserve praise who take criticism with the least impatience.* Pliny the Younger, Epistulae (Letters), Book 7, Letter 20, To Tacitus, Translated by J. B. Firth, 1900, https://www.attalus.org/old/pliny7.html. Accessed May 23, 2025.

[26] Psalm 141:5.

not only from the hand of God who sends it our way, but from the hand of a friend who brings it.

We should never be like the wicked Sodomites[27] or that disrespectful Hebrew,[28] people who more or less spit in the face of their reprovers, not understanding that the men who reproved them were truly the best friends they had. "Who made you a prince and a judge over us?"

David, however, gives us a different response. When Abigail prudently chocked the wheels of his anger, David not only blessed God who sent her and blessed her advice, but he also blessed her! He not only listened to her voice but received her graciously and with honour![29]

Now, there are times when the reprover assumes the fault is greater than it really is, and sometimes the reproof is not given with all the prudence in the world, yet even in those times, meekness will teach us to accept it quietly and to make the best use we can of the correction. Even if we are entirely innocent of the matter of which we are being reproved, the meekness of wisdom teaches us to apply the reproof to some other fault of which our own consciences convict us. We should not fight against the kindness of a reproof, even if it's not done well, and in some situations, mistaken or misplaced.

Now, for those of you who are in positions under authority—children, employees, students—you must with all meekness and submission receive the reproofs of your parents, bosses, and teachers. Their age suggests they have more understanding than you do, and their position gives them an authority over you to which you should offer deference, and under which you should submit by complying to their direction. If not, we say farewell to all order and peace.

The angel rebuked Hagar for fleeing from her mistress, despite the fact that Sarai had dealt harshly with her, and the

---

[27] Genesis 19:9.
[28] Exodus 2:14.
[29] 1 Samuel 25:32-35.

angel even ordered her to return and submit herself to her mistress.[30] "If the anger of the ruler rises against you," and you be reproved for a fault, "do not leave your place," as one under authority, for "calmness will lay great offenses to rest."[31] "If you have been devising evil, put your hand on your mouth"[32] to keep that evil from breaking out in any excessive or inappropriate language.

Meekness teaches us that when a righteous reproof is given, we should not pay as much attention to the one who speaks as to what is spoken.

Reproofs are likely to do us good when we submit meekly to them. They are "like a gold ring or an ornament of gold," when "a listening ear" is offered to "a wise reprover."[33]

Even those in positions of authority should receive reproofs from those under them with meekness, as they would any other gift of kindness and goodwill. Naaman, the man who turned the prophet away in a rage, listened to the reproof his own servants gave him, and he was overruled by the reason offered in their arguments. This, of course, was no more of a criticism to him than it had been to receive instruction from

---

[30] Genesis 16:6-9.
[31] Ecclesiastes 10:4.
[32] Proverbs 30:32.
[33] Proverbs 25:12.

his wife's maid regarding to whom he should turn for a cure for his leprosy.[34]

Meekness teaches us that when a righteous reproof is given, we should not pay as much attention to the one who speaks as to what is spoken.

3. We Must Instruct with Meekness

Ministers are told that they "must not be quarrelsome but kind to everyone," [35] in meekness instructing those who oppose them. Ministers serve the Prince of Peace, [36] they preach the gospel of peace,[37] they are ambassadors of peace,[38] and therefore they must be sure to keep the peace.

The apostles, those Prime-Ministers of the state in Christ's kingdom were not soldiers, nor were they men of strife or quarrels. They were fishermen who worked their jobs with quietness and silence. It is extremely necessary that the leaders of the church be strict governors of their own anger. "Learn from me," says Christ, "for I am gentle and lowly in heart,"[39] and therefore I am fit to teach you. We must "contend," but not in anger or passion! Anger is not the way to contend "for the faith that was once for all delivered to the saints."[40]

When we have assurance that we are proclaiming the truth, we must manage our defence against those who are

---

[34] 2 Kings 5:1-14.
[35] 2 Timothy 2:24-25.
[36] Isaiah 9:6.
[37] Ephesians 6:15.
[38] Possible reference: 2 Corinthians 5:20.
[39] Matthew 11:29.
[40] Jude 1:3.

contrary in a way not to cause the *deceived to be confused*, but the *deception to be confuted.*[41]

Meekness, then, will teach us not to prejudge an issue or to condemn an enemy before hearing their side of the story. Instead, it will teach us to calmly lay out the areas where we disagree, knowing that a truth well laid out is already half confirmed.[42] Meekness will also teach us not to aggravate the issue in an argument, nor to pin on your adversary all the absurd consequences which we think might be inferred from his opinion. Meekness would teach us to judge those who disagree with us from a standpoint of love and kindness, and to endure all the personal attacks that come our way in the argument.

God's purposes do not need the help of our sinful passions which often cause a great deal of damage to the truth we are trying to share. Meekness prevents and cures that intolerance which has so long been the bane of the church, and it contributes a great deal towards the advancement of that happy state in which, despite our little differences of understanding and opinion, the Lord will be one and his name will be one. Large reformations happen in the most wonderful and comfortable manner and are most likely to be built on lasting foundations when meekness stands at the stern of that ship and guides the movements and directions.

When Christ was driving out the money changers from the temple, even though he was moved by a zeal for God's house that consumed him, he still did it with meekness and prudence. This is observed in that he drove out the sheep and oxen, those animals which could be easily caught again, but to those who sold doves, he said, "Take these things away."[43] He did not let the doves loose, sending them flying off into the

---

[41] Simple definition: *to prove something wrong.* SPR Note: I kept some of the original style here in the hopes of maintaining M. Henry's alliteration.

[42] Original: *knowing that a truth well opened is half confirmed.*

[43] John 2:13-17.

sky, for that would have caused loss and resentment in the owners.

Angry, loud, and bitter arguments do not fit with those who claim such a great truth as the gospel, the truth that will win in the end.[44] Our Lord Jesus lived in a very disobedient and perverse generation, yet it is said, "He will not quarrel or cry aloud, nor will anyone hear his voice in the streets."[45] Though Jesus could have broken them as easily as a bruised reed and extinguished them as easily as smoldering wick, yet he will not do that until the day comes when "he brings justice to victory."[46]

Moses dealt with a very stubborn and stiff-necked people, and yet "my teaching," says Moses, will "drop as the rain, my speech distill as the dew."[47] It was not the wind, nor the earthquake, nor the fire that brought Elijah to a calm state— for the Lord was not in them—but a "still small voice." When he heard that, Elijah wrapped his face in his cloak.[48]

In dealing with argumentative people, a spirit of meekness will teach us to consider their emotional state, education, customs, the power their prejudices hold over them, the influence of others on them, and to make allowances accordingly, and not to call, as angry and argumentative people tend to, every false step an apostasy. No, not just that, they tend to call every error and mistake, even every misconstrued word, a heresy and every small crime nothing less than treason and rebellion.

These anger-filled reactions are a means of moving forward that are more likely to irritate and harden people's hearts than to help argumentative people understand and pull back from their contentiousness. I have heard it said, "the

---

[44] SPR Note: Some original versions include the phrase: *without all that adoe* which means *without all that trouble/fuss*.

[45] Matthew 12:19.

[46] Matthew 12:19-21.

[47] Deuteronomy 32:2.

[48] 1 Kings 19:11-13 KJV.

scourge of the tongue has driven many out of the temple but never drove any into it."[49]

4. We Must Offer Our Profession with Meekness

We must also make our profession of the hope that is in us with meekness. Be "prepared to make a defense." You must be ready to make your defence or argument, whether this is before a judge or in everyday life, as there is need, "to anyone who asks you for a reason for the hope that is in you." This is, of course, to be done soberly, not with an attitude of ridicule or mocking, and it is a defence that points to the hope you profess, the hope you wish to be saved by. You must do this "with gentleness and respect."[50]

Notice that it is very consistent with Christian quietness for that quiet spirit to make an appearance when we give our defence of the truth and when we declare our faith openly at any point when we are called to do so. However, it is not meekness to quietly betray and hand over Christ's truths or established ways by remaining silent at times when we are called to speak. That is cowardice! Never meekness! Such a move suggests we are ashamed or afraid to confess our Master! The office of meekness at times such as this is present to direct us as to how and in what manner we might bear our testimony. We should never do this with pride or anger, but with humility and mildness.

Those who desire to successfully confess the truth must first learn to deny themselves. We must give an account of our hope, always maintaining a holy fear that we might miss the

---

[49] SPR Note: I have left this quote in the original wording. I searched for the source of this quote, but I have not been able to find it. I suspect it was simply a familiar saying in M. Henry's time. For that matter, the concept is also quite familiar to us in our times.

[50] 1 Peter 3:15.

opportunity to do so at a crucial moment. When we give a reason for our faith and hope, we must not boast about ourselves or our accomplishments, nor should we ever show contempt or anger towards those who are persecuting us, but remember that "the truth that you have,"[51] the truth that you are about to declare, is also the word of Christ's patience.[52] This means it is the word which must be patiently suffered for, according to the example of him who, with invincible meekness, "made the good confession"[53] before Pontius Pilate. A display of great humility, humbling ourselves before those whom we make our defence, may very well go hand-in-hand with a firm assurance of the truth and a profound glorification of it.[54]

Now, in smaller, less important matters, where even the wisest and best among us are not all in agreement, meekness teaches us not to be too confident that we are right, nor to judge and condemn those who have a difference of opinion from us. It is not as if we, ourselves, are the people, and wisdom itself will die with us![55] Meekness then teaches us to quietly walk according to the light that God has given us, and graciously believe that others do as well, waiting until God will reveal this or that truth to them or us![56]

In situations such as this, let it be enough for us to justify our beliefs,[57] as every man has a right to do, without putting on a judge's robe, declaring judgement, and slamming the gavel down to declare their sentence is set in stone! Why should we all be teachers when we all stumble in so many ways?[58] Is it not

---

[51] 2 Peter 1:12.

[52] Revelation 3:10.

[53] 1 Timothy 6:13.

[54] Original: *A great abasement and diffidence of ourselves may very well consist with a firm assurance of the truth, and a profound veneration for it.*

[55] Job 12:2.

[56] Philippians 3:15.

[57] Original: *Let it in such cases suffice to vindicate ourselves...* Possible Scripture reference: 2 Corinthians 7:11.

[58] James 3:1-2.

true that our place is not to sit as judge, but to stand in defence?[59]

Meekness will, in this way, teach us to manage a personal opinion in which we disagree with others with all possible deference to them. It will help us hold our views lightly, not resenting another's opinion as if their disagreement with us is a personal attack. Instead, we can see it as a kindness from them to help us be better informed.

We must also never be angry when someone challenges the hope we have in Christ. To go through this trial, if we act properly in it, may result in praise, honour, and glory, and our meekness will contribute towards all of this, putting a shine on the surface of it and filling the testimony we share with convincing power. We then will "walk in a manner worthy of the calling to which [we] have been called," when we walk "with all humility and gentleness."[60]

5. We Must Bear Disgrace with Meekness

Disgrace is a branch of that persecution of which all who desire to live godly in Christ Jesus must expect.[61] We must submit to this disgrace with a quiet behaviour and proper conduct, not only when "princes sit plotting against" us[62] but even when the wretches themselves gather "together against," us,[63] and we become the song of the drunkard.[64]

Sometimes it is easier to keep calm in a serious interaction that we knew was coming than in a surprise argument or quick

---

[59] Original: *...and the bar is our place, not the bench?*
[60] Ephesians 4:1-2.
[61] 2 Timothy 3:12.
[62] Psalm 119:23.
[63] Psalm 35:15.
[64] Psalm 69:12.

confrontation.[65] Therefore, even against these minor attacks, it is necessary that meekness should remain on guard. If we are slandered[66] and have all kinds of evil uttered against us falsely,[67] our rule is to not be disturbed at it, nor to repay "reviling for reviling."[68] Now, we may, as we have opportunity, in meekness deny the charge against us, as Hannah did when Eli too-quickly judged her as drunk: "No, my lord... I have drunk neither wine nor strong drink,."[69] But when that is done, we must, without planning any revenge, quietly commit our cause to God who will, sooner or later, prove our righteousness as the light, which is promised in Psalm 37:5-6. Therefore, "fret not yourself" but wait patiently, "refrain from anger, and forsake wrath."[70]

Mr. Dod had a tendency to charm his friends into silence by throwing the following statement at them: "If a dog bark at a sheep, the sheep will not bark at the dog again."[71] When we allow the peace and serenity of our minds to be broken by the attacks of the world, we please our great enemy and do his work for him. For me, to put myself into a rage because another abuses me is similar to scratching the skin on my face to remove the dirt thrown at me by my enemy. When attacks provoke our anger, which leads us to return bitterness for bitterness, we lose the comfort and forfeit the honour and reward which God's promise has set aside for us when we suffer for Christ. Should we suffer so many things for no reason at all?

---

[65] Original: *rencounter.* SPR Note: This word suggests more of a chance meeting than confrontation, but due to the context of this section, this rewrite seemed appropriate.

[66] Some original versions: *If we be nick-named and slandered...*

[67] Matthew 5:11.

[68] 1 Peter 3:9.

[69] 1 Samuel 1:15.

[70] Psalm 37:7-8.

[71] The Gleanings of Heavenly Wisdom: The Sayings of John Dod, p. 26, 1851.

When we respond poorly, we likely give occasion to those who had spoken evil of us falsely to speak evil of us truly, and perhaps the church's reputation [72] suffers more by our impatience than by the attack itself. For what reason do we have the law as well as the pattern and promise of Christ, if not to calm our spirits when we are attacked for doing good? Certainly if we cannot endure a cruel or unkind word for Christ, we won't be able to endure much at all. If we faint or worry on the day of adversity, it is a sign our strength is small. [73]

When attacks provoke our anger, which leads us to return bitterness for bitterness, we lose the comfort and forfeit the honour and reward which God's promise has set aside for us when we suffer for Christ.

We should be satisfied in the knowledge that by our meekness and quietness under attack, we invite God to step into the situation. He has promised he will "with righteousness... judge the poor," the poor in spirit, and will "decide with equity for the meek of the earth." [74] The One who has commanded us to open our mouths for the mute [75] will not himself be silent.

---

[72] Original: *religion.*
[73] Proverbs 24:10.
[74] Isaiah 11:4.
[75] Proverbs 31:8.

And will we not eventually learn that instead of worrying and raging we should rejoice and be exceedingly glad when we "are persecuted for righteousness' sake?"[76] Will we not put these persecutions in our crown as pearls, confident that they will easily pass the judgement when we are blessed with the resurrection of names as well as bodies? In this we have reason to rejoice that we are "counted worthy to suffer dishonor for the name,"[77] that we are honoured to be dishonoured for him who for our sakes endured the cross and despised the shame.[78]

It is one of the laws of meekness to not care at all if we are despised.[79]

By our meekness and quietness under attack, we invite God to step into the situation.

---

[76] Matthew 5:10.

[77] Acts 5:41. *Dominus ipse matedictus est, & tamen solus est Benedictus.* Tertul. de Pattent. cap. 8. Transl: *The Lord Himself was cursed… and yet is He the only Blessed One.* Tertullian, Of Patience, Chapter 8, https://www.newadvent.org/fathers/0325.htm. Accessed May 26, 2025.

[78] Hebrews 12:2.

[79] *Spernere se sperni, transl. to despise being despised.* SPR Note: This is part of a larger quote attributed to St. Philip Neri recorded in Maxims and Sayings of St. Philip Neri. The larger quote is: *Spernere mundum, spernere nullum, spernere se ipsum, spernere se sperni,* Transl. *To despise the world, to despise no person, to despise oneself, to despise being despised.* The concept is to point out four things required to perfectly obtain the gift of humility. To despise being despised doesn't appear to suggest we hate the thought that someone might not like us, but rather that we do not care at all (despise) if someone despises us. http://www.liturgialatina.org/oratorian/maxims.htm. Accessed May 26, 2025. NOTE: Some have attributed this phrase to St. Bernard of Clairvaux.

A Discourse on Meekness

VII

Principles to Apply

For a meek person to truly govern their soul, their judgement must be equipped with proper rules and boundaries, otherwise, they will never be able to keep peace in their hearts. With the proper restraints in place, when we have set these good principles as rules to govern our hearts and influence our reactions, the emotions of the soul will then be able to remain steady, consistent, and constant.

Now,[1] there are some worldly principles by which angry, argumentative people are guided. One such principle is the belief that to forgive one injury *invites* another,[2] and that the

---

[1] NOTE: Some original versions do not include the next three and a half paragraphs until *In this chapter, we will focus on...*

[2] *Veterem ferendo injuriam, invitas novam. P. dict. pub. min.* Rough transl. *By forgiving one injury, you invite another.* SPR Note: It is unclear what *P. dict. pub. min.* refers to. This quote seems to be a common proverb known and used in M. Henry's time. This proverb is also referenced in Thomas Nashe's

forgiveness might justify an adversary's actions. In contrast to this, a meek view might consider that perhaps it is true that the forgiving of one offence might enable us to *endure* the next.

It is also suggested by the world that we must have satisfaction for every wrong done to us. However, in meekness we realize that if we do not find satisfaction for the injury, if the sin is not our fault, we can feel satisfied that we have done what is right, and that is in itself good.

Perhaps it is true that the forgiving of one offense might enable us to endure the next.

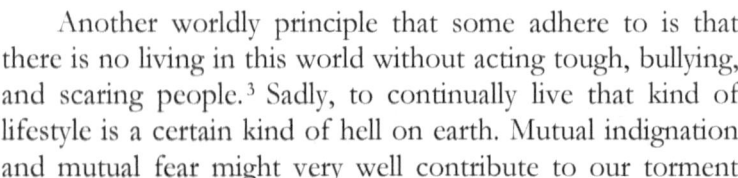

Another worldly principle that some adhere to is that there is no living in this world without acting tough, bullying, and scaring people.[3] Sadly, to continually live that kind of lifestyle is a certain kind of hell on earth. Mutual indignation and mutual fear might very well contribute to our torment from devils and damned spirits.[4]

---

satirical work entitled, *Strange News*. In his work he translates the phrase in a tongue-in-cheek manner as, *One cup of nippitate pulls on another*. http://www.oxford-shakespeare.com/Nashe/Strange_News.pdf. Accessed May 27, 2025.

[3] *Oderint dum metuant.* Transl. *Let them hate, so long as they fear.* SPR Note: This is a quote from Lucius Accius (170-86 BC), I believe from his work, *Atreus*, but this work is lost. This phrase is quoted and discussed by Seneca the Younger (4 BC - AD 65), in his work *On Anger*, Chpt. 20, Section 4. In Seneca's works (On Clemency, approx. 55AD), he considered this phrase the thinking of a tyrant, which is interesting as this phrase had previously been Emperor Caligula's personal motto (AD 37-41).

[4] Possible reference: Matthew 18:34.

However, contrary to these worldly, unhealthy principles, we should treasure the good truths chosen out of the many which could be mentioned in this book. In this chapter, we will focus on truths that are proper for us to use when occasions for meekness arise.

1. Peace Is Found in Meekness

The one who has the sweetest and best peace in their heart is the one who is the greatest master of their own emotions. The comfort found in governing yourself is a much greater comfort than what you can find through others serving you, even if nations bow down to you. It is a sure thing that the worst enemies we can have, if they ever break loose and gain control, are the enemies in our own hearts. Enemies outside your heart can only bring the threat of pain. They can kill the body,[5] but there is no great threat in that to a child of God, as long as the enemies within, our own angry emotions, do not break free and plunge us into the evil of sin. That is the much greater evil![6]

An invasion from far away does not disturb the peace of a kingdom as much as an insurrection at home. Therefore, it is important for us to double our guard where the danger is the greatest. Above all things, we must keep our hearts so that no angry passions can rise up without good reason or without good benefit from their presence. And then if "we are afflicted in every way, but not crushed; perplexed, but not driven to despair,"[7] offended by our fellow-servants, but not offending our Master, criticized by our neighbours, but not by our own consciences, this is the peace of Zion, peace within the walls.[8]

---

[5] Matthew 10:28.

[6] SPR Note: Some original versions do not include this sentence.

[7] 2 Corinthians 4:8-9.

[8] Psalm 122:7.

We have need to pray as one man did, "Lord, deliver me from that evil man, myself,"[9] and then we will be safe enough. The passions that "are at war within you"[10] are the enemies that "wage war against your soul."[11] If this war is won, and those enemies suppressed, whatever other disturbances arise, we will have peace in the soul with grace and mercy from God and from the Lord Jesus.[12]

Nehemiah was aware his enemies desired to upset him when they hired a false prophet to give him a warning and to advise him to selfishly protect himself.[13] It was for the purpose, said Nehemiah, "that I should be afraid and act in this way and sin."[14]

Whatever we lose, we will not lose our peace if only we keep our integrity. Therefore, instead of being anxious to subdue the enemies who lay siege to our lives, let us instead double our guard against the traitors within our own ranks, from where the danger truly lies! Since we cannot prevent the throwing of the fiery darts, we should be careful to have our shield ready with which we can extinguish those darts.[15]

If we don't hurt ourselves, all blessing to God, no enemy in the world can hurt us. Let us keep the peace within our hearts by governing our own angry passions, and then

---

[9] *Liberame à malo isto homine, meipso.* Transl: *Deliver me from that evil man, myself.* SPR Note: This in an unattributed quote, but it is possible M. Henry was quoting a contemporary of himself, John Howe, from his book, *The First General Epistle of St. John the Apostle, Unfolded and Applied,* in which Howe states, *Custodi, libera me de meipso, Deus! Lord, deliver me from myself!* 1865, p. 89, https://ia800308.us.archive.org/24/items/firstgeneralepis00hard/firstgeneralepis00hard.pdf. Accessed May 27, 2025.

[10] James 4:1.

[11] 1 Peter 2:11.

[12] 2 John 1:3.

[13] Original: *advise him to meanly shift for himself.*

[14] Nehemiah 6:13.

[15] Ephesians 6:16.

whatever attacks come our way, we may with the daughter of Zion despise them, scorn them, and shake our heads at them.[16]

We should truly believe that in times of upset and alarm, our strength is to sit still in a holy quietness, composed of mind. "This is rest, give rest to the weary, and this is repose."[17]

2. We All Stumble

In many ways, we all stumble. This is why most of us should not be teachers.[18] If, however, we were to consider the following truths, it would help subdue and moderate our anger at the offences of others.

a. It Is Human Nature to Stumble

Stumbling happens to all of us because it is human nature to stumble.

While we live in this world, we must not expect to dwell with angels or righteous men made perfect. No, we are stuck communicating with creatures who are foolish and corrupt, evil and provoking, and who are under the thumb of passions similar to our own. We must live among people like this, unless we find a way to leave this world.

Do we not then have reason to expect there will be anxious and upsetting experiences in all our relationships and in all the situations we face? The best men have their defects in this imperfect state in which we live. Even those who are enlightened with the saving grace of Jesus Christ only know in part—they still have their blind side. It is a reality that harmony, even amongst the unity of the saints, will sometimes be upset with unharmonious songs. Why then should we be

---

[16] Isaiah 37:22.

[17] Isaiah 28:12.

[18] James 3:2.

surprised and driven to anger and upset when the thing that has upset us is the very thing we expect to see?

The harmony, even amongst the unity of the saints, will sometimes be upset with unharmonious songs.

Instead of growing angry, we should think this way: "Alas, what else could I expect but irritating actions and words from corrupt and fallen men?"

Among such foolish creatures as we are, stumbling will always happen, and why shouldn't I contribute my share of stumblings? The God of heaven gives this as a reason for his patience towards such an upsetting world: it is in their nature to provoke! "I will never again curse the ground because of man, for the intention of man's heart is evil from his youth,"[19] and therefore we should not expect more from humanity.

And with this in mind, he had compassion on Israel: "He remembered that they were but flesh." [20] Not only weak creatures, but sinful and bent on backsliding. "Are grapes gathered from thornbushes?"[21] "I knew that you would surely deal treacherously, and that from birth you were called a rebel."[22]

Should we not be ruled much more by the same understanding? "If you see in a province the oppression of the

---

[19] Genesis 8:21.
[20] Psalm 78:39.
[21] Matthew 7:16.
[22] Isaiah 48:8.

poor and the violation of justice and righteousness," remember what a corrupt creature sinful man is, and then you won't be amazed at it.[23]

We should make use of our understanding of the common weakness and corruption of humankind, not to excuse our own faults, which takes the power out of our repentance and is a silly lie from a deceptive heart, but to excuse the faults of others. This understanding also helps to remove the extremes of our anger and displeasure and preserve the meekness and quietness of our own spirits.

b. We Are Often the Ones Who Stumble

The Apostle puts himself into this number:[24] We all stumble. We all offend God. If we say we do not, we deceive ourselves,[25] and yet even so, he bears with us from day to day and does not keep track of what we do wrong. Our debts to him are talents, and our brother's debts to us are mere pennies.[26]

Consider, then, if God were to be angry with me for every sin against him, just as I am with those who sin against me, what would become of me? Those who hurt me are careless in their actions and perhaps intentional in their offence, but am I not the same way? Absolutely! In fact, am I not a thousand times worse?

Job said that when his servants complained, and he was tempted to be harsh with them, "What then shall I do when God rises up? When he makes inquiry, what shall I answer him?"[27]

---

[23] Ecclesiastes 5:8.
[24] Συνδωλος και αυτος. *Himself a fellow-servant.*
[25] 1 John 1:8.
[26] Matthew 18:21-35.
[27] Job 31:13-14.

Do we not also tend to offend our brothers? Either we *have* offended them, or we *will* offend them. Either way, we need others to *bear*[28] with us, so why shouldn't we *bear* with them?[29] Our rule is, whatever we wish that others would do to us when we offend them, we should do to them when they offend us, for this is the Law and the Prophets.[30] Solomon appeals to our consciences in this regard, "Your heart knows that many times you yourself have cursed others."[31] The repentant remembering of former guilt greatly helps to stifle the passionate resentment of present trouble.

The repentant remembering of former guilt greatly helps to stifle the passionate resentment of present trouble.

---

[28] *Palieonter illalam injuriam toleral, qui pie meminil quod fortasse ad huc habeat in quo dobeal ipse lolerari. That man patiently endures wrong, who piously remembers that perhaps there is something in his conduct, which requires forbearance.* Greg. M. in Job, 1. 5. c.32. Gregory the Great, Morals on the Book of Job, Book 5, Section 45, Chpt. 81. This reference with a different translation can be found here: https://www.lectionarycentral.com/GregoryMoralia/Book05.html. Accessed May 27, 2025.

[29] *Hanc veniam petimusque damusque vicissim. Let us seek and grant pardon alternately.* Horace, Ars Poetica, line 11, trans. A. S. Kline: *I know it: I claim that licence, and grant it in turn.* ToposText digital library. https://topostext.org/work/682.

[30] Matthew 7:12. *Cogitemus alios non facere injuriam, sed reponero.* Transl. *Let us not, I say, suppose that others are doing us a wrong, but are repaying one which we have done them* Sen. Seneca the Younger, De Ira (On Anger), Book II, chapt. 28. https://standardebooks.org/ebooks/seneca/dialogues/aubrey-stewart/text/on-anger. Accessed May 28, 2025.

[31] Ecclesiastes 7:22.

I once read a story about a lazy, rebellious son who dragged his father by the hair of the head to the door of the house. It then calmed the anger of the father when he remembered that he himself had also dragged his own father just as far. In another situation, it seemed to have silenced Adonibezek when he remembered that he had treated others in a similar way to how he was being treated.[32]

c. Men Are God's Hand

"From men by your hand, O Lord," or rather we are tools in his hand, which is his "sword."[33] We must abide by this principle that whatever it is that crosses us or displeases us at any time, God has an overruling hand in it.

David was ruled by this principle when he put up with Shimei's spiteful attacks with such unwavering patience. "Let him curse... because the Lord has said to him, 'Curse David...' Leave him alone... for the Lord has told him to."[34]

This understanding will not only silence our grumblings against God, the author, but also all our arguments with men, the cause of our trouble and irritation. Men's disgraces are God's rebukes, and whoever it is who attacks me, I must understand and declare that in this my Father corrects me.

This understanding quieted the spirit of Job regarding the attacks from the Chaldeans and Sabeans, even though he lived as a king among his troops.[35] His power and control seem to have been maintained when the intruders first broke through, and because of this, he couldn't help but see that his help remained in the gate.[36] Still, we do not find him considering revenge, but instead he calms the disturbance in his own soul

---

[32] Judges 1:7.
[33] Psalm 17:13-14.
[34] 1 Samuel 16:10-11.
[35] Job 29:25.
[36] Job 31:21.

with the understanding of God's sovereign work and involvement,[37] overlooking all the people causing his trouble. If he had focused on the people and on revenge, it would have brought anger into his heart, an upsetting passion, and added that anger to his sorrow. To set that all aside, then, is enough to still the internal storm. "The Lord gave, and the Lord has taken away; blessed be the name of the Lord."[38]

> # We know for certain that we are taking up arms against the king if we take up arms against anyone who is sent by him.

When Job's brethren stood aloof from him, his family and his friends looked scornfully on him as a stranger, and instead of oil, they poured vinegar on his wounds, so that all he could see was the continuation of his suffering,[39] yet even at that point, he saw it as the hand of God: "He has put my brothers far from me."[40] It is a truth that can bring such quiet to our hearts—the Lord help us to add faith to this truth—that every creature is exactly what God intends it to be to us and no more.

While many seek the ruler's favour and perhaps even more people fear the ruler's displeasure, the judgement of every man comes from the Lord alone.[41] If we would only just

---

[37] Original: *sovereign disposal*. SPR Note: This would seem to refer to, considering the archaic meaning and this context, God's habits, and in this case, *his sovereign, trustworthy, work and involvement*.

[38] Job 1:21.

[39] Original: *so that his eye continued in this provocation*.

[40] Job 19:13.

[41] Proverbs 29:26.

see and trust that it is God's hand at work in those things that upset and anger us, surely that would change everything. Since we would then not focus on man but would hold onto the fear of God, this attitude would help to reconcile us to the struggles we face and help suppress all extreme and improper resentments.

When we grumble at the stone, we are actually criticizing the hand that threw it, and in that, we place ourselves under the judgement declared for us and for all who strive against their Creator. We know for certain that we are taking up arms against the king if we take up arms against anyone who is sent by him.

d. We May Grow from the Offense

There is no attack or insult given to us at any time that can't help us grow or improve, and therefore good can come of it. If we have the wisdom of the prudent man which helps to discern our way[42] and all the advantages and opportunities that wisdom provides, we can, despite the intention of those who try to hurt us, gain some real, spiritual benefit for our souls through the hurts and offenses committed against us.

For even these difficult experiences are made to work together for good for those who love God.[43] This response is a holy and happy way of opposing our enemies and resisting evil. The spiritual bee can extract something profitable, for its own purposes, from anything other than a useless weed. Whatever lion might roar against us, we must go on in the strength and spirit of the Lord, just as Samson did. We may find that we can not only tear the lion like we might tear a young goat so that it does not harm us, but we may also find

---

[42] Proverbs 14:8.
[43] Romans 8:28.

we get something to eat out of the eater and something sweet out of the strong.[44]

Many people harm themselves immeasurably as they misinterpret learning opportunities as attacks and respond with anger and displeasure. So, for us, it would benefit us immeasurably if we could learn to interpret attacks as learning opportunities and make use of them for the conviction of our spirits and the humbling of our hearts. Through this, the reproaches of Christ will become true riches for us, greater even than the treasures of Egypt.[45]

There is a story told of a sinner who was cured from his rebellion by the thrust of an enemy's sword,[46] and also another story of a man who was happily converted from drunkenness by being called in reproach a bartender.[47] It is very possible through a hurt or offense we may be enlightened, humbled, or reformed, and we may be brought nearer to God or drawn away from the world. We may be given what we need for repentance or for prayer and praise. All this can come through the hurts committed against us, and we may be brought that much closer to heaven by the very thing that was intended as an attack or insult.[48]

---

[44] Judges 14:5-6, 14.

[45] Hebrews 11:26.

[46] Original: *We are told of an imposthume that was cured with the thrust of an enemy's sword.* SPR Note: The word *imposthume* refers to an abscess in the body, however, one early version I found reinterprets this word as referring to an apostate (one who has walked away from the Christian faith), and the rest of the sentence (comparing this *imposthume* to someone who is converted from alcoholism) suggests the word points to a person who needs the gospel rather than a physical ailment.

[47] Original: *a tippler.*

[48] Ταράσσει τως ανθρωπως ω τα πραγματα αλλα τα περι των πραγ ματων δογματα. *Mortals are made unhappy, not so much by EVENTS as by the OPERATION of their minds upon them.* Epict. Ench. c. 10. Epictetus, Enchiridion, chapter 5, https://classics.mit.edu/Epictetus/epicench.html. Accessed May 29, 2025.

This principle would shift our perspective on injuries and unkindness towards us and would change the very nature of these attacks, teaching us to call them something other than an offense. Whatever people themselves have intended—and it is likely they did not intend or even think of it in such a way[49]—God designed these experiences in our lives for the purpose of yielding the peaceful fruit of righteousness,[50] just as he designs all afflictions for this purpose. Because of this, rather than being angry at the man who intended us harm, we should instead be grateful to the God who intended us good, and then we should strive to respond to his intention!

This understanding kept Joseph at peace with his brothers, though he had plenty reason to fight with them. "You meant evil against me, but God meant it for good."[51] This understanding also satisfied Paul—regarding the thorn in the flesh, that is, the troubles and oppositions he faced from the false apostles, something that hurt him more deeply than all the efforts of the raging persecutors—because he understood that it was intended to keep him humble. This thorn was given to prevent him from "becoming conceited because of the surpassing greatness of the revelations."[52] And what's interesting in this passage is there seems to have been a good effect on him just by mentioning it, for a few lines later, he makes this humble statement: "I am nothing."[53]

If we do not experience some hurts in life or face contempt from other people, we will likely think too highly of ourselves and find we love the world too much. It is through these experiences that we learn not to trust in people. And if we take the time to carefully understand the benefit we can

---

[49] Isaiah 10:7. NOTE: This phrase is not in all original versions: *it is likely he meant not so, neither did his Heart think so.*

[50] Hebrews 12:11.

[51] Genesis 50:20.

[52] 2 Corinthians 12:7.

[53] 2 Corinthians 12:11.

find through these hurts and difficulties, we will also not be so quick to seek revenge for them.

If we do not experience some hurts in life or face contempt from other people, we will likely think too highly of ourselves and find we love the world too much.

e. We Will Often Need to Repent

It is easy to understand that whatever is said in haste today will usually require a thoughtful repentance tomorrow. We find David often regretting what he said in haste. In fact, there was one word in particular said during a time of distress and trouble that disturbed him. The word spoken pointed the finger at Samuel and everyone who had given him any encouragement in terms of his future kingdom. He declared, "All mankind are liars,"[54] and this hasty word bothered him for a long time after. "Whoever makes haste with his feet misses his way."[55]

When anger drives a man to act improperly, we often justify it by saying, "He's a little hasty," as if there really is no harm in it at all, even though we see there actually is harm.[56] However, someone who acts too quickly can do a lot of evil in a short amount of time. What we say or do when we are hot-

---

[54] Psalm 116:11.

[55] Proverbs 19:2.

[56] SPR Note: Some original versions do not include this last phrase.

tempered will need to be unsaid or undone when we have cooled down, or else we end up doing more damage by not addressing the matter.

Now, which one of us is going to do something that we know we're going to have to repent of later? Even an unbeliever who is tempted to commit a sin with serious penalties will find he can resist the temptation when he considers how high a cost it is to repent.[57]

Is repentance really so much fun that we would enthusiastically store up wrath for ourselves on the day of wrath,[58] either God's wrath against us or our own anger at ourselves for our actions? We rarely think how much personal suffering we allow into our lives when we let loose the reins on uncontrolled, extreme anger.

You are angry at someone, and you call him on his actions,[59] ready to hate him and take revenge, but notice how your corrupt nature takes a sick pleasure in it all. Do you not know that all this will eventually come back on you? It will definitely all fall back on you!

You will have to repent of every sin, either here or in a worse place. In other words, you will need to turn all this emotion back on yourself! You will need to be angry at yourself and call yourself on your actions. You will need to call yourself a fool and hate yourself, beating your fists against your chest. If God gives you the grace to repent, take a holy revenge on yourself! This is considered the fruit of true, godly sorrow,[60] and is there anything more uncomfortable than that?

You feel you have a great deal of freedom to rebuke those who are in positions under your authority, and you might even

---

[57] A Cabinet of Choice Jewels, Thomas Brooks, 1669, chapter 8. https://www.gracegems.org/Brooks/a_cabinet_of_choice_jewels2a.htm. Accessed July 3, 2025. Original: ...*he would not buy repentance so dear.*

[58] Romans 2:5.

[59] SPR Note: Some originals include the phrase: *and call them hard names.*

[60] 2 Corinthians 7:11.

speak abusively to them. Such a thing is easy because you know they won't dare to rebuke you back, but don't you fear your own heart will turn on you? Won't your own conscience rebuke you?

Isn't it easier to hear a rebuke from another person, which is something you can avoid, answer, or brush off, than to hear the rebuke of your own conscience? You can't avoid hearing it, so there's no way to downplay it to yourself! When your conscience is active, it will be heard and will tell you in your heart, "in truth we are guilty concerning our brother."[61]

Let this thought calm your spirit when a storm brews inside: remember that by speaking in your anger, you will simply have to repent later. However, as Abigail suggested to David, the bearing and forgiving of a hurt will not be a bother, nor will it cause you any grief later. Let wisdom and grace do what time accomplishes for all of us: let it cool our hot tempers and take the edge off our resentments.

f. God's Way Is Best

When we consider what is truly best for us, we come to realise that what is best for us is the very thing that is most pleasing and acceptable to God. And truthfully, a meek and quiet spirit pleases God. No principle has a more powerful influence on the soul than those things that have to do with God and which bring us to a place where we are acceptable to him.

The woman of Tekoah hinted at this when she begged David for a merciful sentence. "Please let the king invoke the Lord your God."[62] No thought could be more pleasing than that!

Remember how gracious, merciful, and patient God is. Remember how slow to anger, how ready to forgive, and how

---

[61] Genesis 42:21.
[62] 2 Samuel 14:11.

pleased he is to see his people become like him. Remember the eye of your God is on you, remember the love of God towards you, and remember the glory of your God set before you. Remember how important it is for you to be accepted by God and to walk in a manner that is worthy of the relationship you have with him, pleasing him in all ways.

Consider how much meekness and quietness of spirit contributes to your ability to please God as it reflects that beautiful faith established by our Lord Jesus, and as it makes your heart a proper home for the blessed Spirit. "This is good, and it is pleasing in the sight of God our Savior," to "lead a peaceful and quiet life."[63] It is also evidence that we are truly reconciled to God, if we can be a peace with every difficult experience,[64] something that requires a meek response towards everyone who is involved in causing us grief.

St. Augustine explains it well in his commentary on Psalm 122: "Those who please God are the ones who are pleased with God,"[65] and with all he does, whether he does it directly through his own hand or through the hands of men who seek to harm and injure us. If you wish to stand complete in all the will of God, not only with his direct commands but also with all the difficulties he allows to take place in our lives, then you

---

[63] 1 Timothy 2:2-3.

[64] Original: *cordially reconciled to every trying providence.*

[65] *Quis placet Deo? cui Deus placuerit. Those please God that are pleased with him.* SPR Note: This reference points to Augustine's Expositions on the Psalms, specifically Psalm 122, but due to a difference in counting between the Greek Septuagint and the Hebrew Masoretic texts, it appears to be referring to his exposition of Psalm 123, chpt. 2. However, I was unable to find a complete translation of the Latin for that chapter (what I found only translated approximately 1/3 of the chapter). Here is the reference to a portion of the translation: https://www.newadvent.org/fathers/1801123.htm and for those who wish to play around with the Latin, the untranslated text can be found through the following link: https://monumenta.ch/latein/xanfang.php?n=5. Accessed May 29, 2025.

must be willing to say without hesitation, "Let the will of the Lord be done."[66]

If we honestly live with a true respect for God and sincerely desire to be accepted by him, we will find we will, in some measure, be adorned with that meek and quiet spirit which we know to be very precious in the sight of God.[67]

These are the principles that soften our hearts. Everyone who walks according to these rules will have peace and mercy, and no doubt this peace and mercy will also be on all of God's people.

---

[66] Acts 21:14.
[67] 1 Peter 3:4.

VIII

Disciplines to Apply

The laws of our holy faith are so far from contradicting one another that one Christian duty actually strengthens and promotes the next. The fruits of the Spirit are like links in a chain, one holds onto another, and it is the same way with a meek and quiet spirit. The many other graces that we have all contribute towards this meekness.

If you now see how attractive it is to have meekness, will you, because of your desire for it, set yourself on a path to pursue it? Will you seek and pursue it with all wisdom[1]—at the *very least* all wisdom—that you may reach the meekness that comes from wisdom?

---

[1] Proverbs 18:1 KJV.

1. Stop Loving the World

It is time for us to withdraw all affection for the world and everything in it. The more the world is crucified *to* us, the more our corrupt passions will be crucified *in* us. If we wish to live a life that is calm and quiet, we must, by faith, live *above* the stormy regions of this world.

It is guaranteed that everyone who has anything to do with the world will meet with difficult experiences every day as they interact with others, and these interactions will upset and provoke them. And if our affection is set on the things of the world, and if we are overly concerned about them as if they are the most important things, these upsetting experiences will, without a doubt, deeply wound us and enrage the soul.

It is guaranteed that everyone who has anything to do with the world will meet with difficult experiences every day.

And anything that touches our soul in this way, touches us in the apple of our eye.[2] If we overly indulge our appetites with things that please us, our passions will to the same degree be enraged at things that displease us. Therefore, as Christians, whatever you own or have in the world, whether it be a lot or a little, if you value peace and purity in your soul, keep these things you own out of your heart. Every time you allow your affections to grow when it comes to possessions, things you

---

[2] Psalm 17:8. SPR Note: The *apple of the eye* signifies a precious and well protected area.

enjoy, and things you get excited about, keep in mind the disappointment and the upset that you will probably experience as a result of this affection, and let that knowledge restrain you and hold back your improper behaviour.[3]

In the wonderful advice of Epictetus, whatever you enjoy, take the time to consider what it truly is and to approach it with an appropriate level of affection. "If, for example, you are fond of a specific ceramic cup, remind yourself that it is only ceramic cups in general of which you are fond. Then, if it breaks, you will not be disturbed."[4]

Those who idolize things in this world will be terribly upset if they are challenged in that area of their lives. The money which Micah's mother had was her god before it was formed into the shape of a graven or molten image. If it hadn't been, the loss of it would not have led to a curse, as it seems to have.[5]

Those who are "greedy for unjust gain" trouble their own hearts as well as their own households.[6] They end up a burden to themselves and a dread to all those around them. "Those who desire to be rich," who set their hearts on it no matter

---

[3] SPR Note: Some original versions do not include this last phrase: *and let that knowledge restrain you and hold back your improper behaviour.*

[4] Αν χυτραν σεργης, μεμνησο οτι χυτραν ςεργεις, κατεάγεισης γαρ αυτης κ ταραχθηση - *If thou art in love with a China cup, or a Venice glass, love it as a piece of brittle ware, and then the breaking of it will be no great offence.* Enchiridion, Epictetus. Translation in the text above is from Elizabeth Carter, https://classics.mit.edu/Epictetus/epicench.html. Accessed June 1, 2025. SPR Note: Some originals do not include the quote, merely the general statement (which references Epictetus' writings up until the phrase *appropriate level of affection.*)

[5] Judges 17:2. Bishop Joseph Hall, D.D., Contemplations on the Historical Passages of the Old and New Testaments, 1858, page 137, https://ia802300.us.archive.org/29/items/contemplationson00halluoft/c ontemplationson00halluoft.pdf. Accessed June 1, 2025.

[6] Proverbs 15:27.

what, cannot help but fall into "senseless and harmful desires."[7]

And those who serve their own appetites, who are not happy with anything unless it is extremely fun, who are like the "most tender and refined woman among you, who would not venture to set the sole of her foot on the ground because she is so delicate and tender,"[8] leave themselves quite open to everything that can upset them, and they cannot, without growing angry, endure any kind of disappointment.

Therefore, Plutarch, a great moralist, gives us some wonderful advice for the preservation of meekness.[9] He tells us not to get caught up in food, clothes, or social events, because "those who need but little are not disappointed of much."[10] If we could simply learn to deny ourselves when it comes to all these things, we would not be so quickly hurt when someone challenges us in these areas.

Therefore, the start of this lesson in Christ's school is for us to deny ourselves and then take up our cross.[11] We must also crush[12] any deep inner desire for the praise of men as such desire is entirely inconsistent with true happiness. If we learn how to not base our value on their approval, we will simply never be upset by their disapproval. St. Paul was able to put up with the criticisms of others with such meekness because he did not build his life on the opinions of other people. In fact,

---

[7] 1 Timothy 6:9.

[8] Deuteronomy 28:56.

[9] *Ne quere molliane tibi contingant dura. - Ask not whether your allotment will be pleasing or painful.* Phurant. SPR Note: In my research, I was unable to figure out what *Phurant* refers to. It may be a misspelling of *Plutarch.*

[10] Plutarch, On the Control of Anger, https://penelope.uchicago.edu/ Thayer/E/Roman/Texts/Plutarch/Moralia/De_cohibenda_ira*.html. Accessed June 1, 2025.

[11] Matthew 16:24.

[12] Original: *mortify.*

he considered it "a very small thing [to be] judged" by man's opinion.[13]

2. Repent Often

We must repent often of all our sinful, extreme emotions, and renew our commitment to stand against them. If, when we reflect on our reactions to others, we find we grow angry, and that is something we hate, we might not be so quick to fall back into it.

If repentance is genuine and deep and grounded in true remorse and humility,[14] it prepares the soul to endure insults with a great deal of patience. We all have plenty of reason to live a life of repentance, and if we live out this repentance, we will find we cannot help but live a quiet life, for no one can speak worse things about a truly penitent man than he himself speaks about himself. Call him a fool, an insult many would think is justification for a fight, and the humble soul can endure it patiently, thinking, "Yes, I am a fool, and I've called myself that many times." "Surely I am too stupid to be a man. I have not the understanding of a man."[15]

Repentance prepares us in a special way for meekness when it latches onto any improper and unacceptable passion that has taken hold of our hearts. When we experience godly sorrow for our former sins, that sorrow will bring about in us a heart that seeks not to fall into that sin again.[16]

If others are angry with us—either without reason or when they grow excessively angry—am I not simply getting back what I deserve for my own even worse anger? Pile the sorrow and shame onto your own consciences, aggravate the sin and stack up a heavy burden on your shoulders for it, and

---

[13] 1 Corinthians 4:3.

[14] SPR Note: Some original versions include the phrase: *is very meekening.*

[15] Proverbs 30:2.

[16] 2 Corinthians 7:9-10.

you will find that the burned child, especially when the burn still hurts, will dread the fire.[17]

Once we repent of our former unquiet spirit, we must commit ourselves with a firm resolution in the strength of the grace of Jesus Christ to be more mild and gentle in the future. Declare that you will guard your ways so as not to sin with your tongue as you have in the past, and just like David, remember often that you have committed yourself to this path.[18]

A strong commitment towards meekness will go far when it comes to the task of sanding down our rough edges.

A strong commitment towards meekness will go far when it comes to the task of sanding down our rough edges and helping us to quietly endure the greatest upsets. This commitment, this resolution is like a bit and bridle to the horse and mule, those creatures that have no real understanding. It may be a good reminder every morning for us to pull back on our affections, hoping to keep the peace. As we welcome Christ into our lives through faith and meditation, we should then commit to not allowing any unruly emotions to upset or misdirect our love.[19]

---

[17] See Job 42:6. SPR Note: this is not a quote from Job 42:6, but it is instead a reference to a common saying, *a burnt child dreads the fire*. This saying was first recorded in English in the mid 13th century.

[18] Psalm 39:1.

[19] Original: *stir up or awake our love*. This would be a reference to Song of Solomon 2:7 & 8:4.

3. Stay Away from Irritations

Avoid those things that irritate you and stand guard against them. Since we are so quick to sin in this way, we need to pray and practice the words, "lead us not into temptation."[20]

People who look for a fight, who fish for an argument and dig up mischief are enemies both towards themselves and their own peace,[21] and they are enemies to society as a whole. But meek and quiet people, on the other hand, who diligently avoid those things which provoke others even when they are justified by reacting in such a manner, those meek and quiet people will act as if there has been no offense.

If you don't want to be angry, you need to wink at those things that upset people or learn to see those things in a positive light. The advice of the wise man is very helpful in this regard: "Do not take to heart all the things that people say, lest you hear your servant cursing you."[22] It is better, of course, not to hear it at all, unless you can hear it patiently and not be angry to the point of sinning.[23]

There is a common story of a man named Cotys who, when given a cupboard full of beautiful glasses, thanked the friend who sent them, paid the messenger who brought the gift, and then intentionally broke every last one. He did this to

---

[20] Matthew 6:13.

[21] *Facilius est excludere perniciosa quàm regere, et non admittere quàm odmisse mederari. - It is easier to exclude pernicious passions than to govern them; not to admit them, than to manage them when admitted.* Seneca, Letters to Lucilius, 85.9. https://topostext.org/work/736. Accessed June 2, 2025. The translation on this website (translated by Richard Mott Gummere 1883–1969, Loeb Classical Library 1917-25) is as follows: *For it is easier to stop them in the beginning than to control them when they gather force.*

[22] Ecclesiastes 7:21.

[23] *Non vis esse iracundes? Ne sis curiosus. - Wouldst thou avoid anger! Suppress curiosity.* Seneca the Younger, On Anger, Book 3, chapt. 11, translation from the following citation: *Would you not be irascible? then be not inquisitive.* https://standardebooks.org/ebooks/seneca/dialogues/aubrey-stewart/text/on-anger. Accessed June 3, 2025.

avoid the possibility that at a later point he might break one by accident and grow angry.

There is also a story told by Dion that points out Julius Caesar's honour. In this story, Caesar receives many letters from Pompey, but he refused to read them since Pompey was an enemy, and he knew he was likely to find things in those letters that would worsen their quarrel.[24] In Dr. Reynolds's words,[25] "he chose rather to make a fire on his hearth than in his heart."[26]

Now, since "briers and thorns are with" us, and we "sit on scorpions,"[27] and since "temptations to sin are sure to come,"[28] we need to be extra careful. As careful as we might be if we were to carry a candle among barrels of gunpowder. We need to put in the effort to have clear consciences, careful neither to offend others nor to resent the offenses of others.

Whenever we are anywhere, be it for business or pleasure, and we anticipate conflict or upset, we need to be extra careful and cautious. David says, "I will guard my mouth with a muzzle."[29] In other words, while the wicked are near me, we must take special care and be extra diligent. Through

---

[24] Cassius Dio's Roman History, Book 41, chapt. 62, https://penelope.uchicago.edu/Thayer/e/roman/texts/cassius_dio/41*.html. Accessed June 3, 2025.

[25] The Whole Works of the Right Rev. Edward Reynolds, Lord Bishop of Norwich, Volume 6, p. 242. https://books.google.ca/books?id=NjsQAAAAYAAJ&pg. Accessed June 3, 2025.

[26] *De non existentibus & non apparrentibus eadem est ratio. Keep the injury out of sight, and it will be out of mind.* This Latin quote is from Sir Edward Coke's Reports, Part V, xxii. A literal translation appears to be closer to, *The reasoning is the same concerning things not apparent as concerning things not existing.* M. Henry's translation appears to be a moralistic interpretation of this legal concept. https://babel.hathitrust.org/cgi/pt?id=chi.26887276&seq=1. Accessed June 3, 2025.

[27] Ezekiel 2:6.

[28] Matthew 18:7; Luke 17:1.

[29] Psalm 39:1.

repetition, we will be able to confirm our meekness and turn it into a habit.

Plutarch speaks to this matter as well. He suggests:

> ...to set some time to ourselves for special strictness; so many days or weeks, in which, whatever provocations do occur, we will not suffer ourselves to be disturbed by them.[30]

So Plutarch supposes, then, that extreme, habitual anger can be conquered and subdued by taking small steps to eradicate it. However, the grace of faith has the greatest influence on establishing a quiet spirit. Faith establishes the mercy of God, the meekness of Christ, the love of the Spirit, the commands of the Word, the promises of the covenant, and the peace and quietness of heaven.[31] Faith, then, is the approved shield with which we can extinguish all the flaming darts of the evil one,[32] and all the efforts of his followers.

4. Learn to Pause

Learn to pause. Take a moment. This is a good rule to live by not only in our relationship with God, but as we interact with people. "Be not rash with your mouth, nor let your heart be hasty to utter a word."[33]

Whenever we are upset by someone or something, taking a short break may be as much to our advantage as a wrongly

---

[30] Plutarch, On the Control of Anger. SPR Note: This is not a direct quote, but appears to be taken from chapters 3 and 16 of Plutarch's work. https://penelope.uchicago.edu/Thayer/E/Roman/Texts/Plutarch/Moralia/De_cohibenda_ira*.html. Accessed June 3, 2025.

[31] Original: *upper world.*

[32] Ephesians 6:16.

[33] Ecclesiastes 5:2.

timed break in other circumstances might be dangerous. "Good sense makes one slow to anger."[34]

"I would beat you," said Socrates to his servant, "if I were not angry,"[35] but "he who has a hasty temper," who jumps on board with his anger the moment it rises, "exalts folly."[36]

Our rational mind, our reason, is there to govern our extreme emotions, but in doing so, we must give time to act and not allow the tongue to run ahead of our reason. There are those who have recommended that when we are provoked to anger, we should take as much time to consider our actions as it takes to recite the entire alphabet. Others have thought it better to repeat the Lord's prayer, and perhaps by the time we are at the fifth petition, "forgive us our debts, as we have forgiven our debtors,"[37] we may find we are calm.

It is a good rule to think twice before we speak once,[38] for "whoever makes haste with his feet misses his way."[39] A great statesman in Queen Elizabeth's court famously said, "Take time, and we shall have done the sooner."[40] Not only that, but there is nothing lost when we defer our anger. There is nothing

---

[34] Proverbs 19:11.

[35] *Caedisse nisi iratus essem.* Seneca makes this the Saying of Socrates while Ambrose *De Officiis, On the Duties of the Clergy*, and others ascribe it to Archytas Terentium. Ambrose references this in chpt. 94 of *On the Duties of the Clergy.* https://www.newadvent.org/fathers/34011.htm. Accessed June 3, 2025.

[36] Proverbs 14:29.

[37] Matthew 6:12.

[38] SPR Note: While this is a common proverb or familiar concept to all of us, it appears to be attributed to Thomas Fuller's Gnomologia (1732), although I can't find it in his work.

[39] Proverbs 19:2.

[40] SPR Note: It is difficult to know who this *statesman* is. I have narrowed it down to two possibilities, Sir Francis Walsingham and Lord Burghley (William Cecil), however, it could be someone else entirely. Additional NOTE: *Polest paena dilata exigi, non potest exacta revocari. Punishment though deferred, may be inflicted; but when once inflicted, it cannot be recalled.* Seneca, De Ira, On Anger, chapt. 22, https://standardbooks.org/ebooks/Seneca /dialogues/aubrey-stewart/text/on-anger, Accessed June 3, 2025.

done or said in our wrath that is not better said and done in meekness.

5. Ask God to Develop Meekness in You

You should pray and ask God to develop in you this wonderful grace of meekness and quietness of spirit. It is a part of that beauty which he places on the soul, and it only comes to us when we seek it. If anyone lacks this meekness of wisdom, let him ask it of God who gives freely and does not blame us for our foolishness.[41] When we, at any time, start to be argumentative and unquiet, we must pray to him who calms the raging sea, seeking that grace that establishes the heart.

When David's heart grew angry, the first words that came from him came in the form of a prayer.[42] When we are surprised by something that upsets us, and feel ourselves growing angry, we have a wonderful solution available to us. It is not merely a quick diversion, but a divine cure, to lift our hearts to God in prayer for grace and strength to resist and overcome the temptation. "Lord, keep my heart and my mouth quiet!"[43] "Let your requests [in this matter] be made known to God. And the peace of God… will guard your hearts and minds."[44]

You may be quick to complain about those around you who are not very meek, but you have more reason to complain about the anger and rage within you. What others have are merely thorns in a hedge, but the anger inside you is a thorn in

---

[41] James 1:5.

[42] Psalm 39:3-4.

[43] Original: *Lord, keep me quiet now.*

[44] Philippians 4:6-7.

the flesh. And if you seek the Lord, as Paul did, with an active, unwavering faith, you will also receive sufficient grace.[45]

6. Evaluate Your Growth Often

We should often take the time to evaluate our own growth and proficiency in this grace of meekness.[46] Take a look at how much control you have over your anger and emotions and see what improvements you have made in the area of meekness.

Every day you will face things that can anger you, things that have historically upset you. These experiences give you the opportunity to evaluate where you are at with this matter. Do you find you are less likely to fall into anger? When you do grow angry, are you moved by it less than you were in times past. Are you slower to allow yourself to be upset by those things that cause hurt, and are you less focused on your resentments? Is the little kingdom that is your mind quieter and more at peace than it has been in the past, and those parts of you that are not content, are those areas finding themselves lacking in strength and held down by your own restraint?

If you have grown in this area, it is a positive thing, and it is a good sign that the soul is healthy and doing well. Every night we should take some time to evaluate if we have been quiet throughout the day. We will find we sleep better if we have. Let your conscience always keep up a constant investigation in the soul with a mandate given by the Judge of Heaven and Earth to inquire and bring to light all evidence of lack of restraint, disorderliness, and breaches of peace within us. Let nothing be left hidden due to your own desires, affections, or self-love, and do not allow anything brought to

---

[45] 2 Corinthians 12:7-9.

[46] Αρξαι απο των μικρων, εκχειται το ελαδιον; κλεπτεται αιναριον ; επιλεγε, οτι τοσυτυ πωλειται απαθεια τοσυτω ατραξια. *Begin with little things, Is the oil spilt? Is a trifling quantity of wine stolen? Say to thyself, "So much tranquillity is sold, so much composure."* Epictetus, Enchiridion, chpt. 12, https://classics.mit.edu/Epictetus/epicench.html. Accessed June 4, 2025.

light to be ignored, instead, go after it according to the law of God!

It is the clearest sign of righteous living to keep ourselves from guilt.

Those who, due to personality, age, or health, are easily angered, hasty, and unquiet people[47] are given an opportunity by meekness and gentleness to discover both the truth and the strength of grace in general. It is the clearest sign of righteous living to keep ourselves from guilt,[48] and so, if the children of God produce these fruits of the Spirit in their old age, which is a time when men are most contrary and stubborn, it shows that they are not only living righteously, but rather that the "Lord is upright," in whose strength they stand, that he is their "rock,[49] and there is no unrighteousness in him."[50]

7. Enjoy Spending Time with Meek People

To grow in this grace of meekness, it is wise to spend time in the company of meek and quiet people. Solomon considers this to be a way to protect ourselves against foolish emotions when he encourages us to "make no friendship with a man given to anger… lest you learn his ways."[51]

---

[47] Not all original versions include *easily angered* (original: *hot*) or *unquiet*.
[48] Psalm 18:23.
[49] Some originals add: *in whom they have cast anchor.*
[50] Psalm 92:14-15.
[51] Proverbs 22:24-25.

When a neighbour's heart is enraged, it is time to protect your own.[52] People, however, are social creatures, and we are cut out for interacting with others. Since we need to have friends and to be with others, it is wise to choose to have fellowship with those who are meek and quiet. This way, we will learn their ways, for their way is a good way.

The wolf is not a good friend for the lamb, nor is the leopard a good friend for the young goat, not unless they forget how to "hurt and destroy."[53] The people we hang around change us to be like them,[54] and we are very likely to, without even knowing it, grow to be like those we enjoy spending time with. Because of this, let the quiet of the land be the ones we choose to spend time with, especially when it comes to those with whom we have ongoing friendships and with those who are our closest of friends.

> ## We are very likely to, without even knowing it, grow to be like those we enjoy spending time with.

Pay attention to others, noting how sweet and admirable the meekness in their lives is. See how those who have control over their extreme emotions enjoy themselves as if it is, for them, heaven on earth, and strive to copy their example. There are those who take pleasure in wild company and are never

---

[52] SPR Note: Some original versions state: When *thy neighbour's house is on fire, it is time to look to thy own*, while others state, *When thy neighbour's heart is on fire, it is time to look to thy own*. I suspect the latter version is the original.

[53] Isaiah 11:6-9.

[54] 1 Corinthians 15:33.

happy unless they are surrounded by noise and shouting.[55] Certainly the real heaven will not be much of a heaven to people like that, for God's heaven is a calm and quiet place. The only noise there will be what is sweet and harmonious.

8. Reflect on the Cross

It is important for us to reflect[56] on the cross of our Lord Jesus. If we simply knew more about Jesus Christ and him crucified, we would experience more of the fellowship of his sufferings.[57] Reflect often on how he suffered and in what manner. See him led as a lamb to the slaughter,[58] and arm yourself with the same mind.[59] Consider why he suffered and for what purpose so that you may not in any way contradict the plans and purposes of your dying Saviour, nor that you might receive his grace in vain.[60]

Christ died as the great peacemaker, the One who was to take down all dividing walls, to quench all threatening flames, and to reconcile his followers, not only to God, but to one another by the slaying of all enemies.[61] The apostle often suggests a faith-filled view of the sufferings of Christ to be a powerful means to overcome all sinful and extreme anger and emotions.[62] Those who wish to display the meek and humble life of Christ in their mortal bodies must always carry with them "the death of Jesus."[63]

---

[55] SPR Note: This could also be understood as *brawls and shouting.*

[56] Original: *study,* which can carry the concept of *reflection, pursuit,* or *scrutiny.*

[57] Philippians 3:10 KJV.

[58] Isaiah 53:7.

[59] Philippians 2:5-8.

[60] 2 Corinthians 6:1.

[61] Ephesians 2:14-16.

[62] Ephesians 5:2; Philippians 2:5.

[63] 2 Corinthians 4:10.

The ordinance of the Lord's supper, that wonderful time when we proclaim the Lord's death and the new testament in his blood,[64] must be made full use of for this blessed purpose of a love-feast,[65] a time when all our sinful passions must be set aside,[66] and as a marriage-feast, where the adorning of a meek and quiet spirit is a worthy part of the wedding attire.[67] The forgiving of hurts and reconciliation with our brothers and sisters is not only a necessary part of our preparation for this ordinance, but it is also clear proof that we are benefiting from it.

If God has in that place spoken peace to us, we should not go out from there and speak war to our brothers and sisters. The year of release under the Law, which put an end to all legal actions, disputes, and arguments, started on the close of the day of atonement when the Jubilee-Trumpet sounded.[68]

9. Consider Your End

In your minds, spend much time reflecting and considering the reality of the dark and silent grave. You will often face things in this life that will disturb and upset you, and you will have to endure a great deal of conflict. Think about how quiet death will make you and how incapable you will be in the grave of resenting or resisting hurts. This body which you put so much effort into caring for will soon be easy prey for the worm which will feed sweetly on it. You will soon be out of reach of provocation in the place where "the wicked cease from troubling,"[69] and where their envy and hatred will be dead forevermore.

---

[64] 1 Corinthians 11:26.

[65] 1 Corinthians 11:22; Jude 1:12.

[66] Colossians 3:8.

[67] Revelation 19:6-9.

[68] Leviticus 25; Deuteronomy 15:1-11. SPR Note: Not all original versions include this paragraph.

[69] Job 3:17-19.

Is not having a quiet spirit the best way to prepare for that quiet state? Consider how all these things which upset us now will look when we stare death in the face! How small and inconsiderable they will seem to someone who is about to step into eternity. Think, "why should I resent an insult or hurt if I am nothing more than a worm today, and tomorrow, worm food?"

They say, when bees fight, you can part them by throwing dust among them.[70]

> Yet all those dreadful deeds, this dreadful fray
> A cast of scatter'd dust will soon allay.[71]

A little sprinkling of the dust of the grave on the edge of the cliff on which we stand would go a long way towards quieting our spirits and ending our quarrels. One day soon, death will quiet us. Let grace quiet us now. When David's heart was angry within him, he prayed, "Oh Lord, make me know my end."[72]

---

[70] SPR Note: Not all original versions include this sentence and the following quote.

[71] Virg. Geor. lib 4. *Hi motus animorum atque hæc certamina tanta, Pulveris exigui jactu compressa quiescunt.* Dryden. SPR Note: This reference points to the writings of Publius Vergilius Maro (70–19 BC) from his work named, The Georgics (poetry). The translation (in this footnote) is from Book 4 of John Dryden's translation of the work entitled, Virgil's Georgics. https://quod.lib.umich.edu/e/eebo/A65112.0001.001/1:18.4?rgn=div2;view=fulltext. Accessed June 4, 2025.

[72] Psalm 39:3-4.

Conclusion

In conclusion, I do not think there is any way I could succeed in this task better than to explain this to you:

> Meekness is extremely effective in bringing about the comfort and rest of our own souls and making our lives sweet and pleasant. If you are wise in this matter, you will enjoy the benefit of it.

What I have set out to do in this discourse is to persuade you to not be your own tormentor, but instead to rule your own emotions so that they may not cause you to suffer. This adornment that I have laid out before you is clearly both excellent and lovely. Will you put it on and wear it, so that everyone will know you are a disciple of Christ?[1] Will you take it on yourself so that you may be found to be one of the sheep

---

[1] *Chrysostom argues excellently from the easiness of forgiving, and being meek:* T. ευχολωτερον της οργης αφειναι, μη γαρ μαχραν αποδημιαν ετι τειλαθαι, μη χρηματα δαπανησαι, αρχει θελησαι μονον, &c. *What is more easy than to dismiss anger: for there is no necessity of sending to a remote country, nor to spend money; to will is all that is wanting.* Hom. 19. ad. Pop. Antioch. This is one of Epictetus's τα ε--' ημιν—*things within our power.* SPR Note: This quote is from The Homilies of St. John Chrysostom on the Statutes or To the People of Antioch, Oxford, 1842, Homily XX, chapt. 6, p. 329, https://dn790009.ca.archive.org/0/items/homiliesofsjohnc09john/homil iesofsjohnc09john.pdf. Accessed June 4, 2025. For the Epictetus quote above, Epictetus, Enchiridion, chpt. 1, https://classics.mit.edu/Epictetus/ epicench.html. Accessed June 4, 2025.

on the right hand, on that great day, when Christ's angels will gather up everything evil from out of his kingdom and remove it? Everyone understands that meekness is a good thing, but in this regard, as in many other situations, honesty is applauded yet neglected.[2]

Love is commended by all, and yet the love of many grows cold. Everyone who does not desire to be self-condemned should practice the things they find praiseworthy. As there is no way I think I could succeed more in this endeavour than by laying out the simple benefit of meekness, it is also quite easy to see if I have succeeded in this task. This tree will be known by its fruit.[3]

There are countless times almost every day which call for the exercise of this grace of meekness, and because of that, the benefit we receive from meekness will quickly be made known to us, as well as to everyone with whom we interact. Our meekness and quietness are easier to see and be evaluated than even our love towards God, our faith in Christ, and those other graces which are experienced primarily between us and God.

Should we then decide to show everyone in all our interactions with others that we have truly benefited by this simple discourse? Should we display our meekness so that our relatives, neighbours, and everyone we interact with may see a change in us for the better and recognize that we have been with Jesus?[4]

We should never let the effects of meekness wear off, but whether we live or die, we must ensure we are found to be among the quiet in the land.[5] We all wish to see quiet families,

---

[2] *Probitus laudatur & alget.* Juvenal's *Satires*, Satire I, line 74. https://web.ics.purdue.edu/~rauhn/Hist_416/hist420/JuvenalSatirespdf.pdf. Accessed June 4, 2025.

[3] Matthew 12:33.

[4] Acts 4:13.

[5] Psalms 35:20.

quiet churches, quiet neighbourhoods, and quiet nations. It will only be this way if there are quiet hearts.

My friends, I truly hope and trust God has spoken to you powerfully through this book.

The LORD bless you and keep you; the LORD make his face to shine upon you and be gracious to you; the LORD lift up his countenance upon you and give you peace.

Numbers 6:24-26

A Discourse on Meekness

Authors Quoted in the Text

The following list is just a little information on the many people quoted in this book. I have placed these names in alphabetical order (as best as I could considering the variety of style of their names) and added *when* they lived, *where* they lived (although many moved around a great deal), and *what* they did.

Augustine of Hippo
       Lived: 354 – 430 AD
       Bishop of Hippo
       Theologian, Philosopher

Andrea Alciato
       Lived: 1492 – 1550 AD
       Bourges, France
       Jurist, Writer, Humanist, University Teacher (Law)

Ambrose of Milan
       Lived: approx. 340 – 397 AD
       Milan, Italy
       Theologian, Mentor of Augustine of Hippo

A Discourse on Meekness

St. Thomas Aquinas
    Lived: approx. 1225 – 1274 AD
    Paris, France
    Famous Scholastic, Theologian

Richard Baxter ("Mr. Baxter")
    Lived: 1615 – 1691 AD
    England
    Puritan Church Leader, Theologian, Writer

Thomas Brooks
    Lived: 1608 – 1680 AD
    England
    Non-Conformist Puritan Preacher

John Calvin
    Lived: 1509 – 1564 AD
    Geneva, Switzerland
    Theologian, Reformer

Cassius Dio
    Lived: 165 – 235 AD
    Rome (and Nicaea)
    Roman Historian

John Chrysostom (John Golden-Mouth)
    Lived: approx. 347 – 407 AD
    Constantinople
    Archbishop of Constantinople, Preacher

Bernard of Clairvaux
    Lived: 1090 – 1153 AD
    Dijon, France
    Cistercian Monk, Abbot, Mystic, Preacher

Sir Edward Coke
    Lived: 1552 – 1634 AD
    London, England
    Judge, Jurist, Politician

Ralph Cudworth
    Lived: 1617 – 1688 AD
    Cambridge, England
    Theologian, Philosopher

John Dod ("Mr. Dod")
    Lived: 1549 – 1645 AD
    Cambridge, England
    Puritan Minister, Author

Diogenes the Cynic
    Lived: approx. 412 – approx. 323 BC
    Athens, Greece
    Philosopher

Epictetus
    Lived: 50 – 135 AD
    Nicopolis, Greece
    Philosopher

Gregory the Great (Pope Gregory I)
    Lived: approx. 540 – 605 AD
    Rome, Italy
    Pope, Initiated the first large scale mission to reach the Anglo-Saxons (sending Augustine of Canterbury)

Hugo Grotius
    Lived: 1583 – 1645 AD
    Paris, France
    Dutch Philosopher, Political Teacher, Theologian

A Discourse on Meekness

Lord Matthew Hale
	Lived: 1609 – 1676 AD
	Alderley, Gloucestershire (England)
	Barrister, Judge

Bishop Joseph Hall
	Lived: 1574 – 1656 AD
	Halsted, Essex (England)
	Bishop

Dr. Henry Hammond
	Lived: 1605 – 1660
	Westwood, Worcestershire (England)
	Archdeacon of Chichester, Clergyman, Biblical Scholar

Quintus Horatius Flaccus (Horace)
	Lived: 65 BC – 8 BC
	Rome
	Roman Poet

John Howe
	Lived: 1630 – 1705 AD
	Great Torrington, Devon (England)
	Puritan Theologian, Preacher, Writer, Chaplain to Oliver Cromwell

Juvenal (Decimus Junius Juvenalis)
	Lived: approx. 55 – approx. 127 AD
	Rome, Italy
	Poet, Creator of the phrase, "bread and circuses"

Flavius Josephus (Born Yosef ben Matityahu)
	Lived: 37 – 100 AD
	Jerusalem/Rome
	Jewish Historian, Priest, Scholar

Thomas Linacre
  Lived: 1460 – 1524 AD
  London, England
  Scholar, Priest, Physician

Joannes Lorinus (Jean Lorin)
  Lived: 1559 – 1634 AD
  Avignon, France
  Jesuit Scholar, Theologian, Writer

Lucius Accius
  Lived: 170 – 86 BC
  Pisaurum (Pesaro), Italy
  Roman Tragic Poet, Literary Scholar

Martin Luther
  Lived: 1483 – 1546 AD
  Wittenberg, Germany
  Priest, Theologian, Seminal Figure in the Protestant Reformation

Abraham Maimonides (Avraham ben ha-Rambam)
  Lived: 1186 – 1237 AD
  Fustat, Egypt
  Jewish Philosopher, Court Physician, Scholar

St. Philip Neri
  Lived: 1515 – 1595 AD
  Rome, Italy
  Italian Catholic Priest

John Norris ("Mr. Norris")
  Lived: 1657 – 1711 AD
  Bemerton, Wiltshire (England)
  Clergyman, Philosopher, Poet, Unrelated to Chuck

A Discourse on Meekness

Johannes Œcolampadius
> Lived: 1482 – 1531 AD
> Basel, Switzerland
> Reformer, Theologian

Bishop Simon Patrick
> Lived: 1626 – 1707 AD
> Cambridgeshire, England
> English Bishop, Biblical Commentator

Katherine Phillips (The Matchless Orinda)
> Lived: approx. 1631 – 1664 AD
> London, England
> Anglo-Welsh Poet, Translator

Pliny the Younger (Gaius Plinius Caecilius Secundus)
> Lived: 61 – 113 AD
> Rome, Italy
> Roman Author, Magistrate, Governor

Plutarch
> Lived: 46 – 120 AD
> Boeotia, Greece
> Greek Biographer, Moralist, Writer

Bishop John Prideaux
> Lived: 1578 – 1650 AD
> Worcester, England
> Bishop, Theologian, Oxford Professor

Rev. Dr. Edward Reynolds
> Lived: 1599 – 1676
> Norwich, England
> Bishop, Theologian, Preacher

Samuel Rutherford
  Lived: Approx. 1600 – 1661
  Scotland
  Presbyterian Pastor, Theologian

Seneca the Younger (Lucius Annaeus Seneca)
  Lived: 4 BC – 65 AD
  Rome, Italy
  Stoic Philosopher, Writer

Bishop Nicholas Stratford
  Lived: 1633 – 1708 AD
  Chester, England
  Bishop

Jeremy Taylor
  Lived: 1613 – 1667 AD
  London, England
  Bishop, Theologian, Devotional Writer

Tertullian
  Lived: 155 – 220 AD
  Carthage, Africa (Tunisia)
  Author, Theologian, Latin Church Father

John Tillotson
  Lived: 1630 – 1694 AD
  Canterbury, England
  Archbishop, Preacher

Immanuel Tremellius
  Lived: 1510 – 1580 AD
  Cambridge, England
  Italian Bible (Hebrew) Translator

Pilgrim's Progress available in *Rewalked*, Original version, and with Study Guide and Helps

A Discourse on Meekness available in a *Rewalked* and an Original Annotated Edition.

Rewalked Online

About the Author

Shawn P. Robinson has a passion for teaching God's Word and seeing people grow in their faith. He has had the privilege of serving in Christian ministry as an Associate Pastor, Lead Pastor, and as a Church Planter.

In 2017, a viral infection in his brain pulled him from pastoral ministry, changing the course of his life from a focus on ministry to trying to recover. Eventually, Shawn's health forced him to step down from his pastoral role. Amidst the illness, Shawn began to write a children's book for his sons and from that grew a passion for writing fiction, which has proven to be an exciting blessing from God during a time when Shawn can no longer serve in vocational ministry.

As Shawn continued to write fiction, learning to trust the Lord in this new direction of life, he quickly found joy both in sharing stories and in sharing gospel allegories.

In time, the Lord laid it on Shawn's heart to create a modern-day rewrite of Pilgrim's Progress, one which might not only remain faithful to the original but also be presented in a more contemporary narrative format, hopefully opening up the story to a new generation. With this, Shawn set out to provide study guides with deep and challenging questions based on a Pilgrim's Progress study he offered to his church years before.

Shawn has a Bachelor of Arts in Christian Studies from Briercrest Bible College in Saskatchewan and a Master of Divinity from Carey Theological College in British Columbia. Shawn is ordained with the Fellowship of Evangelical Baptist Churches in Ontario, Canada. He and his wife and two sons live in Southwestern Ontario.

Books by
Shawn P. B. Robinson

Christian Discipleship

Pilgrim's Progress *Rewalked*
Pilgrim's Progress *Rewalked* with Study Guide
Pilgrim's Progress Annotated Original with Study Guide
A Discourse on Meekness and Quietness of Spirit *Rewalked*

Adult Fiction (Sci-fi & Fantasy)

The Ridge Series (3 books)
ADA: An Anthology of Short Stories

YA Fiction (Fantasy, Sci-fi, Dystopian)

The Sevordine Chronicles (5 Books)
Greks (2 Books)—Coming Soon
The Modder's Run (2 Books)—Coming Soon

Books for Younger Readers

Jerry the Squirrel (4 Books)
Arestana Series (3 Books)
Annalynn the Canadian Spy Series (6 Books)
Activity Books (2 Books)

www.shawnpbrobinson.com/books

www.ingramcontent.com/pod-product-compliance
Lightning Source LLC
Chambersburg PA
CBHW030921120626
46554CB00001B/223